Saoud's Dictionary of Recursive Literary Language
English-English-Arab

Saoud's Dictionary of Recursive Literary Language English-English-Arabic

By Saoud S. Salamah

Saoud's Dictionary of Recursive Literary Language
English-English-Arabic

Dedicated to the loving memory of my dear mother Haoula
Alghadban
RIP

About The Author

Saoud is a stateless guitarist born in 1995. Despite the iniquitous and unfortunate statelessness that stifled his life from a young age, Saoud has been muddling through the hardships with all his might. Composing music, publishing books, translating, and becoming a certified bodybuilding specialist, are only a few accomplishments among many others. The omnivorous consumer of arts, has published *100 Pieces of Me*, a collection of poems which was his first publication. *The Fruit of My Groin & Other Short Stories*, which received warm approbation from its readers succeeding his first work. His third published book is this dictionary (*Saoud's Dictionary of Recursive Literary Language English-English-Arabic*) which took him a week to finish. There are other translation efforts that were unjustifiably unaccredited to him, however, Saoud is currently working on his fourth publication and first novel ever, anticipated to reach the market by the end of the year 2024.

About The Book

Saoud's Dictionary of Recursive Literary Language, as farcical as the name is, wasn't supposed to be published as a dictionary nor in any other printed form. The dictionary, which encompasses 1378 entries, was merely scrawled in a notebook for personal reference by the author himself. A long list of words and short phrases that he (Saoud) garnered over the years through the surfing of books for personal leisure. As a learner of English as a second language, with a penchant for classical literature, Saoud picked up these words and had them itched in his notebook as they kept resurfacing in different books. From the Italian poems of Dante, to the Russian pen of Dostoevsky, and to the German laconic aphorisms of Nietzsche, this dictionary offers the recursive literary language found in the English translated works of the greats.

Saoud's Dictionary of Recursive Literary Language, which was initially called "Saoud's Notes" before the idea of publishing it as a dictionary was gestated, provides 1378 entries, words and phrases ranging from all parts of speech, and organized in an alphabetical order. Each word is followed by a brief definition, a list of synonyms, a meaningful sentence to give a clearer understanding, and finally, the Arabic translation of it. This dictionary can be used by both native English speakers to acquire more lexis, and speakers of English as a secondary language who wish to be more linguistically equipped. Reading this dictionary and familiarizing oneself with the words it offers, is conducive to the honing of one's mental lexicon.

A a

abasement The action or fact of abasing or being abased; humiliation or degradation. Humiliation, degradation, belittlement His constant abasement by his superiors led him to quit his job. إِذْلَال

abate (of something perceived as hostile, threatening, or negative) become less intense or widespread. Subside, diminish, decrease The storm suddenly abated, leaving a calm sea in its wake. يَخْفِت

abatement The ending, reduction, or lessening of something. Decrease, reduction, diminution There was an abatement in the fighting as both sides were exhausted. تَخْفِيف

abbot the head or superior of a community of monks in a monastery Prior, superior, head monk, leader, spiritual leaderThe abbot of the monastery guided the monks with wisdom and compassion, ensuring the community thrived in their spiritual journey. رَئِيس الدَّيْر

abdicate formally give up a position of power or responsibility, especially a throne or leadership role. Renounce, relinquish, resign, step down, surrender, vacate After ruling for over two decades, the king decided to abdicate the throne in favor of his son. يَتَنَازَل

abeyance a state of temporary disuse or suspension. Suspension, dormancy, inactivity, postponement, hiatus The construction project was put

in abeyance until the legal disputes were resolved.
تَوَقُّف مُؤَقَّت

abjection   a state of being cast down or brought low; a condition of wretchedness, degradation, or humiliation.   Degradation, humiliation, wretchedness, misery, dejection   The novel explores the theme of abjection through its depiction of the protagonist's fall from grace and subsequent life of misery.   ذُلّ

ablution   the act of washing oneself, often used for the ritual washing in religious practices.   Washing, cleansing, purification, bathing, lavation   Before entering the mosque, he performed his ablution to purify himself for prayer.   وُضُوء

abnegation   the act of renouncing or rejecting something, often a belief, desire, or personal interest.   Renunciation, self-denial, self-sacrifice, rejection, relinquishment   Her life of abnegation and service to others was admired by everyone in the community.   تَنَازُل

abode a place of residence; a home.   Dwelling, residence, home, house, domicile   After years of traveling, they finally found a peaceful abode in the countryside.   مَسْكَن

abrasive   a substance used for grinding, polishing, or cleaning a hard surface. It can also refer to a person or manner that is harsh and unkind. Harsh, rough, caustic, grating, coarse   The abrasive cleaner effectively removed the rust from the metal surface, but its strong smell was quite unpleasant.   مَادَّة كَاشِطَة

abrogation   the act of repealing or abolishing a law, right, or formal agreement.   Repeal, abolition, annulment, cancellation, nullification The abrogation of the outdated law was seen as a positive step towards modernizing the legal system.   إِلْغَاء

absconded   to leave hurriedly and secretly, typically to avoid detection or arrest, often with something of value. Fled, escaped, bolted, ran away, departed   The suspect absconded from the police custody, leaving the officers bewildered.   فَرَّ هَارِبًا

abseiling   also known as rappelling, is the activity of descending a rock face or steep slope using a rope secured to a fixed point above.   Rappelling, descending on a rope, rope climbing The adventurers enjoyed abseiling down the cliff, taking in the breathtaking view as they descended.   التَّسَلُّق بِحَبْل

abstemious   describes someone who abstains or exercises restraint, especially in the consumption of food or alcohol.   Temperate, moderate, restrained, self-disciplined, sober Despite the lavish buffet, she remained abstemious, opting for a light salad and water.   مُعْتَدِل

abstemiousness   refers to the quality or state of being abstemious, which means showing restraint, especially in the consumption of food or drink.   Moderation, temperance, self-discipline, restraint, sobriety   His abstemiousness in diet and lifestyle contributed to his excellent health and longevity.   اِعْتِدَال

abstention   The act of abstaining or refraining from something.   abstinence, refraining, forbearance   His abstention from voting was a form of silent protest.   امْتِناع

abstinence   refers to the voluntary restraint from indulging in certain activities, especially those that are considered pleasurable or habitual, such as abstaining from food, drink, or sexual activity for religious, health, or personal reasons. Self-denial, refraining, temperance, restraint The monk practiced abstinence from worldly pleasures as part of his spiritual discipline.   الاٴمْتِزَاع

accede to agree to a demand, request, or treaty; to consent or yield to something.   Agree, consent, accept, comply, assent   After much negotiation, the government finally acceded to the protesters' demands for higher wages. وَافَق

accentuate   to emphasize or make more noticeable.   Emphasize, highlight, underscore, stress, spotlight   She used a bold font to accentuate the key points in her presentation slides. يُبرِز

acclimatize   to become accustomed to a new climate or environment.   Adapt, adjust, accommodate, familiarize, acclimate It took a few days for the mountaineers to acclimatize to the high altitude before they could continue their ascent.   تَأَقْلَمَ

accosted   to approach and address someone boldly or aggressively, often in an unwelcome or confrontational manner.   Confronted, approached, intercepted, buttonholed, hailed   She felt uneasy when she was accosted by a stranger in the dimly lit alley. اِعْتَرَضَ

accoutrements   refer to additional items of dress or equipment, often used in a particular activity or profession.   Equipment, gear, paraphernalia, accessories, outfit   The photographer packed all the necessary accoutrements—lenses, tripod, and filters—for the outdoor shoot. مَعَدَّات

acquiesce   to accept or comply with something reluctantly but without protest.   Agree, consent, yield, accept, comply Despite his reservations, he decided to acquiesce to their decision for the sake of maintaining harmony within the team. وافَق

acquiescence   the act of accepting or complying with something reluctantly but without protest.   Agreement, consent, compliance, acceptance, submission   His acquiescence to the new company policy was evident, though he privately disagreed with it. الرِّضا بِالتَّراضي

acquittal   a legal verdict that declares a person accused of a crime to be not guilty. Exoneration, vindication, clearance, absolution, liberation The jury's acquittal of the defendant was met with relief and celebration by his family and supporters. بَراءَة

acrimony   bitterness or harshness in speech, manner, or behavior, especially in a dispute or conflict.   Bitterness, hostility, animosity, resentment, rancor The divorce proceedings were marked by acrimony, making it difficult for the couple to reach a settlement amicably. حَدِيد

acuity keenness or sharpness, especially of thought, vision, or hearing.   Sharpness, keenness, acuteness, sensitivity, perceptiveness   His mental acuity allowed him to solve complex problems with ease. حِدَّة

acumen   the ability to make good judgments and quick decisions, typically in a particular domain, such as business or finance.   Insight, shrewdness, astuteness, discernment, intelligence   Her business acumen helped the company navigate through the challenging economic conditions. بَرَاعَة

acute 1. Sharp or severe: Refers to something intense or severe, often used to describe pain, illness, or problems. 2. Keen or perceptive: Refers to mental acuteness or sharpness of perception. 3. Having a sharp angle: Refers to angles less than 90 degrees in geometry.   Intense, severe, piercing, Perceptive, astute, discerning, Oblique, sharp-angled   1. The patient was experiencing acute pain in his lower back. 2. His acute observation skills allowed him to detect subtle changes in the market. 3. The acute angle formed by the two intersecting lines measured less than 90 degrees.   حاد

addle-headed   describes someone who is confused, muddled, or lacking in clear thinking or understanding.   Confused, muddled, bewildered, befuddled, perplexed   His addle-headed response to the question indicated that he hadn't understood the instructions. غَبِي

adduce   to cite as evidence or justification in support of an argument or claim.   Present, cite, quote, mention, offer The researcher adduced compelling data from various studies to support her hypothesis. قَدَّم

adept describes someone who is very skilled or proficient in a particular area or activity.   Skilled, proficient, expert, capable, competent   She is adept at playing the piano, effortlessly performing complex pieces. ماهِر

adjudication the legal or formal process of resolving a dispute or settling a case by making a judgment or decision.   Judgment, decision, ruling, verdict, arbitration   The adjudication of the land dispute took several months due to the complexity of the legal issues involved. الحُكم

adjudicators are individuals or officials responsible for making judgments or decisions, especially in a formal or official capacity, such as in a competition or legal context.   Judges, arbitrators, referees, examiners, assessors   The panel of adjudicators evaluated the contestants' performances and selected the winner based on predefined criteria. الحُكّام

adjuration is a solemn or earnest urging or advising, often accompanied by a strong appeal to someone to do something. Entreaty, appeal, plea, request, petition The priest's adjuration to the congregation to show compassion and kindness resonated deeply with the listeners. تَوْجِيهُ الذَّصريحَة

adrift floating without being moored or anchored, or metaphorically, to be without direction or guidance. Floating, drifting, unmoored, directionless, aimless After the storm, the boat was left adrift in the open sea, its crew struggling to regain control. طَاف

advent the arrival or coming of a notable person, thing, or event, especially one that is awaited or anticipated. Arrival, coming, appearance, emergence, onset The advent of the internet revolutionized how people communicate and access information worldwide. مَجِيء

adverted to refer to something or call attention to something. Mentioned, referred, alluded, noted During the meeting, she adverted to the previous year's financial report to highlight the company's growth. أَشَار

affability refers to the quality of being friendly, pleasant, and easy to talk to. Friendliness, geniality, amiability, cordiality Her affability made her a favorite among the guests, who found her approachable and warm. لُطْف

affectation   Affectation is behavior, speech, or writing that is artificial and designed to impress.
Pretentiousness, artificiality, pretense, ostentation   His British accent seemed like an affectation, given that he had never lived in the UK.
تَصَدُّع

affianced   to be engaged to be married. Engaged, betrothed, promised, pledged They announced to their families that they were affianced and planned to marry the following spring. مَخْطُوب

affinity   a natural liking for or attraction to a person, thing, idea, etc., or a similarity of characteristics suggesting a relationship.   Liking, attraction, kinship, similarity   She felt an immediate affinity for the new colleague, sensing they shared similar interests and values. انْجِذَاب

affront   an action or remark that causes outrage or offense.   Insult, offense, indignity, slight   His rude comments were taken as a personal affront by everyone in the meeting.   إهَانَة
aforethought   thinking about or planning something beforehand, often used in the context of something done deliberately or with premeditation.
Premeditation, forethought, planning, intention
The jury found that the crime was committed with malice aforethought.
تَخْطِيط مُسْبَق

anfractuous   winding, twisting, or full of bends and turns.   Twisted, winding, meandering, serpentine   The hikers followed the anfractuous path through the dense forest, enjoying the challenge of its twists and turns. مُلْتَوٍ

aggregate a whole formed by combining several (typically disparate) elements. It can also mean to collect or gather into a mass or whole. Total, sum, collection, conglomerate The survey results were aggregated to provide a comprehensive overview of the community's opinions. مَجْمُوع

aggregated the past tense or past participle form of the verb "aggregate." It means to have been collected or gathered into a mass or whole. Collected, gathered, amassed, compiled The data was aggregated from various sources to create a comprehensive report on consumer trends. تَجَمَّع

ajar slightly open, often referring to a door or a window that is not fully closed. Partly open, slightly open, unclosed She left the window ajar to let in some fresh air during the night. مُفَتَّح

akin related by blood or having similar qualities or characteristics. Related, similar, alike, comparable Their love for literature was akin to a family tradition, passed down through generations. مُشَابِه

alabaster A fine-grained, translucent form of gypsum, typically white, used for carving. gypsum, calcite, marble The statue was carved from a single piece of alabaster. المرمر

albeit   means although, even though, or despite the fact that.   Although, though, even though, notwithstanding   She decided to accept the job offer, albeit reluctantly, due to the attractive salary package.   رَغْم

alcove   a small recessed section of a room, typically used for seating or placing furniture. Niche, recess, bay, nook   She loved to read in the cozy alcove by the window, surrounded by sunlight and cushions.   مُغَارَة

alimony   a court-ordered allowance that one spouse pays to the other during separation or after divorce, usually for financial support. Spousal support, maintenance, financial support   After their divorce, he was required to pay alimony to his ex-wife until she found a stable job.   النَفَقَة

alacrity   a cheerful readiness or willingness to do something, often characterized by promptness and eagerness.   Promptness, eagerness, enthusiasm, willingness   She accepted the challenge with great alacrity, eager to prove herself capable of handling difficult tasks. السُرّعة

allocution   a formal speech or address, often delivered by a judge to a defendant after conviction or by a leader to a group.   Address, speech, discourse, lecture   The judge delivered a stern allocution to the convicted criminal, emphasizing the consequences of their actions.   خُطْبَة

allotment   a portion or share of something that is allocated or assigned to someone.   Allocation, portion, share, assignment   Each participant received an equal allotment of time to present their ideas during the meeting. تَخْصِيص

alluring   describes something that is attractive, charming, or tempting, often in a mysterious or enticing way.   Charming, captivating, enticing, seductive   The alluring music and dim lighting created a romantic atmosphere in the restaurant. مُغْرٍّ

allurement   something that entices or attracts, often in a seductive or charming manner. Attraction, lure, temptation, enticement   The offer of a luxurious vacation package was an allurement that she found hard to resist. إغْرَاء

amalgamation   the process of combining or merging multiple things into a single unit, often used in contexts like business mergers, cultural integration, or mixing substances.   Combination, merger, fusion, integration   The amalgamation of the two companies resulted in a stronger market presence and increased efficiency.   اخْتِلاط

amatory   romantic or sexual love, typically used to describe expressions, literature, or actions associated with love affairs.   Romantic, loving, passionate, affectionate   The poet's amatory verses captivated readers with their deep emotional intensity and longing. عَاطِفِي

ambivalent   having mixed feelings or contradictory attitudes towards something or someone.   Conflicted, uncertain, undecided, equivocal   She felt ambivalent about the job offer because it offered great opportunities but required moving away from her family.   مُتَرَدِّد

amelioration   the act of making something better or improving a situation or condition.   Improvement, enhancement, betterment, upgrading   The amelioration of working conditions led to increased productivity and employee satisfaction.   تَحْسين

amenable   describes someone who is willing to cooperate or be influenced by others, typically in a positive or compliant manner.Cooperative, compliant, agreeable, willing   He proved to be amenable to suggestions for improving the project, showing flexibility in his approach.   مُسْتَعِد

amiable   someone who is friendly, pleasant, and likable in disposition or character.   Friendly, affable, genial, pleasant   Her amiable personality made it easy for her to make friends wherever she went.   مُدَرَّب

amicable   describes relations or agreements that are characterized by goodwill and a lack of hostility.   Friendly, cordial, peaceful, cooperative   After the negotiations, they reached an amicable agreement that satisfied both parties.   وَدّي

amorous   describes being strongly attracted to or showing love or sexual desire towards someone.   Romantic, passionate, affectionate, loving

They exchanged amorous glances across the room, unable to hide their mutual attraction. عَاطِفي

amorphous   something that lacks a definite shape, form, or structure, often referring to something vague or indistinct.   Shapeless, formless, indefinite, vague   The concept of beauty is often considered amorphous and subjective, varying greatly among individuals.   غَيْر مُنْتَظَم

amphibious   something or someone that can function both on land and in water.   Aquatic, amphibian, waterborne   Amphibious vehicles are designed to travel across various terrains, including both land and water.   مُزْدَوَج القُوَّة-بَرِّ مَائِي

ample   plentiful or enough in size, amount, or capacity.   Plentiful, abundant, sufficient, generous   The hotel room had ample space for a family of four, with room to spare.   وَفِير

amulet   an object, typically a small ornament or charm, that is believed to protect against evil, harm, or danger.   Talisman, charm, token, fetish   She wore an amulet around her neck, believing it would bring her luck and protect her from negative energies. تَعْوِيذَة-تَمِيمَة-رُقْيَة

anachronism   something that is placed in an incorrect historical time period, or something that is out of place in time.   Misplacement, incongruity, antiquity, incongruence   The use of a rotary phone in a modern movie would be considered an anachronism. تَأْوِيل زَمَانِي-مُفَارَقَة تَارِيخِيَّة

analogues   things that are comparable or similar in certain respects but may be different in others.   Counterparts, equivalents, parallels, resemblances In biology, the wings of bats and birds are analogues for flight, despite their different structures and evolutionary origins   المُمَاثِلات

anathema   something or someone that is intensely disliked or loathed, often considered cursed or denounced.   Abomination, curse, detestation, abhorrence   In some cultures, failure is seen as an anathema, while in others it's considered a necessary part of growth. لَعْنَة

anathematized   something or someone that has been cursed, condemned, or denounced formally, often in a religious or formal context.   Cursed, condemned, denounced, excommunicated   The heretic was anathematized by the church for his controversial teachings.   مَلَعُون

androgyny   a person having both male and female characteristics or qualities, or something that is both masculine and feminine in nature.   Androgynous, hermaphroditic, intersex   The fashion designer's collection featured androgyny clothing that blurred traditional gender boundaries.   أَنْدْرُوجِيْن

androit   means skillful, clever, or adept in using one's hands or mind. Skillful, adept, proficient, competent   She was known for her adroit handling of difficult situations, always finding creative solutions.   مَاهِر

annexation   the act of taking over or adding territory, usually by force or through a legal process.
Incorporation, seizure, occupation, acquisition
The annexation of the neighboring province sparked international controversy and diplomatic tensions.   ضَمّ

annuity   a fixed sum of money paid to someone annually, typically for the rest of their life or for a specified number of years, often used in insurance or retirement planning.   Pension, allowance, stipend, incomeShe received an annuity from her late husband's insurance policy, ensuring financial stability in her retirement years.   مَعَاش

anomaly   something that deviates from what is standard, normal, or expected.   Irregularity, deviation, exception, oddity   The sudden drop in temperature in the middle of summer was an anomaly that surprised meteorologists.   استِثْناء

antagonism   active hostility or opposition between individuals, groups, or ideas. Hostility, opposition, conflict, rivalry There was a clear sense of antagonism between the two political parties during the debate.   تَعَارُض

antebellum   the period before a war, especially the American Civil War.   Pre-war, pre-Civil War   The antebellum era in the United States was marked by significant social, economic, and political changes.   قَبْلَ الحَرْب

antenatal   the period before childbirth, typically used to describe medical care or activities related to pregnancy.   Prenatal, before birth, gravid Regular antenatal check-ups are important to monitor the health of both the mother and the baby during pregnancy. قَبْلَ الوِلاَدَة

anthropophagy   the practice of eating human flesh, usually in a ritualistic or cultural context.   Cannibalism Historically, some cultures have engaged in anthropophagy as part of religious rituals or under extreme conditions of survival. أَكْلُ لَحْمِ البَشَر

antics   playful, silly, or funny actions or behavior.   Pranks, capers, escapades, frolics The children's playful antics kept everyone entertained at the family gathering. أَفْعَالٌ هَزْلِيَّة

antipathy   a strong feeling of dislike or aversion towards someone or something.   Aversion, hatred, hostility, animosity There was mutual antipathy between the two rival teams, evident in their fierce competition. كَرَاهِيَة

antiquated   something that is old-fashioned, outdated, or no longer in use. Obsolete, outmoded, archaic, old-fashioned The company's antiquated software system was replaced with a more efficient and modern solution. قَدِيم

antiquity   the ancient past, especially the period of history before the Middle Ages.   Ancient times, antiqueness, classical period Archaeologists unearthed

artifacts from antiquity that shed light on early
civilizations. العُصُور القَدِيمَة

aphorism   a concise and memorable statement
expressing a general truth or principle.   Adage,
maxim, proverb, saying   "Actions speak louder
than words" is a well-known aphorism that emphasizes
the importance of deeds over mere promises. قَوْلٌ
مَأثُور

aphoristic   a style of writing or speech that is
concise and expresses a general truth or principle in a
memorable way.   Pithy, concise, terse, succinct
     His aphoristic style of writing captivated readers
with its clarity and depth of insight. مَأثُور

aphrodisiac A food, drink, or drug that stimulates
sexual desire. Love potion, stimulant, enhancer   The
ancient Greeks believed that certain herbs acted as
aphrodisiacs. مُثِيرٌ لِلْغَرَائِز

apocryphal   describes something that is of doubtful
authenticity, often referring to a story or statement that
is widely circulated as being true but is probably
fictitious or exaggerated.   Fictitious, fabricated,
legendary, mythical   The apocryphal tale of the
haunted house spread quickly through the
neighborhood, despite no credible evidence supporting
it. مَلْوُف-مُخْتَلَق

apogee   the highest or most distant point; the
culmination or climax of something. Peak, summit,
zenith, culmination   Winning the championship

marked the apogee of her career as an athlete.
ذُرْوَة

apoplectic   someone who is overcome with anger or extremely furious, often to the point of being unable to speak or control their emotions.   Furious, enraged, incensed, livid He was apoplectic when he discovered that his car had been towed despite having parked legally. غَضْبَان

Apostrophising   the act of addressing or speaking directly to someone or something, especially in a rhetorical or emotional manner, often involving apostrophes (').   Addressing, speaking to, invoking, hailing   In his speech, the president was seen apostrophizing the nation's founders, praising their vision and courage.   الخُطَاب-يُنَاجي

appalling   causing shock, dismay, or horror due to its extremely bad or unpleasant nature.   Shocking, horrifying, dreadful, atrocious The news of the earthquake's aftermath was utterly appalling, with widespread destruction and loss of life.   مُرَوَّع

appease   to pacify or satisfy someone by acceding to their demands, often to maintain peace or avoid conflict.   Placate, pacify, mollify, calm The government attempted to appease the protesters by promising reforms to address their grievances.
يُهَدِّئ-اِسْتَرْضَى

appellate   a court or legal proceeding where a higher court reviews the decision of a lower court.   Reviewing, revising, examining   The appellate court overturned the lower court's decision, citing procedural errors. استِدُنَافِي

apprehensive describes feeling anxious or fearful about something that may happen. Anxious, worried, concerned, uneasy She was apprehensive about the upcoming exam, unsure if she had studied enough. قَلِق

apprise to inform or notify someone of something. Inform, notify, advise, brief He quickly apprised his team of the new project deadlines. أَخْبَر

approbation approval or praise, especially when given officially or publicly. Approval, acclaim, praise, commendation The manager's approbation of their hard work boosted team morale. اعْتِمَاد

arcane something understood or known by only a few people, often obscure or mysterious. Obscure, esoteric, mysterious, cryptic The professor's lectures often delved into arcane theories that fascinated his advanced students. غَامِض-مُلْغَز-سِرِّي

ardently having strong feelings or enthusiasm towards something, often shown passionately. Passionately, fervently, intensely, zealously She ardently supported the cause, dedicating countless hours to volunteering. بِشَغَف

armaments weapons and military equipment used by a country or organization. Weapons, artillery, munitions, military hardware The country invested heavily in developing advanced armaments to strengthen its defense capabilities. التَسَلُّح

armistice   a temporary suspension of hostilities or fighting between opposing forces, typically agreed upon during a war to negotiate peace terms.   Truce, ceasefire, peace agreement The armistice signed in 1918 marked the end of World War I. هُدْن

artel   historically refers to a cooperative association of workers in Russia, typically in agriculture or industry, where members shared resources and profits.   Cooperative, collective, association In the early 20th century, artels played a crucial role in Russia's economy, providing a communal structure for labor and resources. جمعية عمالية

ascetic   a person who practices severe self-discipline and abstention from worldly pleasures, often for religious or spiritual reasons.   Austere, abstinent, self-denying, disciplined   The ascetic monk lived a simple life of prayer, meditation, and minimal possessions. زاهد

askance   to look at or regard something with suspicion, distrust, or disapproval.   Skeptically, suspiciously, distrustfully, doubtfully She looked askance at the new proposal, unsure of its feasibility and potential risks. يِرْشَك

assailant   a person who attacks someone physically or verbally. Attacker, aggressor, assailor, perpetrator   The police apprehended the assailant shortly after the robbery attempt. المُهَاجِم

asseverates   to assert or declare something solemnly and emphatically.   Assert, declare, affirm, maintain   The professor asseverated the importance of critical thinking in academic research.   يُؤَكِّد

assiduity   great care and persistent effort, often applied to tasks or duties.   Diligence, perseverance, dedication, attentiveness   Her assiduity in studying paid off when she achieved the highest score in the class. الإجتهاد

assiduous   someone who is diligent, careful, and hardworking, especially in carrying out tasks or duties.   Diligent, conscientious, meticulous, thorough   She was known for her assiduous attention to detail, ensuring every aspect of the project was flawless.   مُجتَهِد

assiduously   in a manner that shows great care, attention, and effort, often applied diligently to tasks or duties. Diligently, conscientiously, meticulously, industriously   She worked assiduously to complete the project ahead of schedule.   يِجِدّ

assuage   to make an unpleasant feeling, such as pain or worry, less intense or severe.Alleviate, ease, relieve, mitigate   He tried to assuage her fears by reassuring her that everything would be fine.   يُخَفِّف

asunder   into parts, apart, or separate. Apart, separate, divided, split   The earthquake tore the building asunder, leaving it in ruins. مُنْفَصِل

astride   sitting or standing with a leg on either side of something.   Straddling, sitting astraddle, spanning   The cowboy sat astride his horse, ready to ride into the sunset.   عَلَى جَانِبَي

astute   someone who is clever, sharp-witted, and perceptive in understanding situations or people.   Shrewd, clever, sharp, insightful   Her astute observations about market trends helped her make profitable investments.   حَذِيف

atavism   refers to the reappearance of a trait in an organism that has been absent for several generations, often due to a reversion to an earlier ancestral type.   Throwback, regression, reversion   The presence of a tail in some humans is considered an atavism, reflecting evolutionary traits from our distant ancestors.   اِلعَوْدُ إِلَى السَّلَف

atonement   the act of making amends for wrongdoing or sins, often through restitution, apology, or penance.   Reparation, redemption, penance, expiation   He sought atonement for his mistakes by volunteering at a homeless shelter.   التَّكْفِير

attunement   the process of bringing into harmony or alignment, often in terms of understanding or sensitivity.   Harmony, alignment, synchronization, rapport   Effective leaders strive for attunement with their teams' needs and motivations.   التَّوَافُق

audacious   describes someone who is bold, daring, or willing to take risks in a confident or fearless way.

Bold, daring, adventurous, fearless   His audacious plan to climb Mount Everest without oxygen captured the world's attention.   جَرِيء

auspicious   something that suggests a positive outcome or success, often indicating favorable circumstances or good luck. Promising, favorable, propitious, fortunate   The team's win at the start of the season was an auspicious sign for their future performance. مُبَشِّر

autodidactic someone who is self-taught, having acquired knowledge or skills on their own without formal instruction.   Self-taught, self-educated, self-trained   He became proficient in programming through autodidactic learning using online resources and tutorials. ذَاتُيّ التَّعَلُّم

avarice   extreme greed for wealth or material gain, often to the detriment of others. Greed, covetousness, rapacity, cupidity   His avarice led him to exploit his employees for greater profits. طُمُع

avaricious   someone who has an extreme desire for wealth and is greedy, often to the point of exploiting others. Greed, rapacious, covetous, grasping   The avaricious businessman cared only about increasing his profits, regardless of the consequences to others. طَمَّاع

averse   a strong feeling of dislike or opposition towards something.   Hostile, opposed, disinclined, reluctant   She was averse to the idea of moving to a new city away from her family and friends. مُعَارِض

avowal   an open declaration or acknowledgment of something, often a belief, intention, or feeling.

Assertion, declaration, affirmation, proclamation

His avowal of love for her took her by surprise, but it filled her with joy.   اِعتِراف-إقرار

B b

bairn a Scottish and Northern English dialect term that means a child or a son or daughter. Child, youngster, kid   She watched her bairn play happily in the garden. صَغِير

balderdash   senseless or exaggerated talk or writing; nonsense or rubbish. Nonsense, gibberish, drivel, twaddle   The article was filled with balderdash, making it difficult to discern any factual information. سَقْسَطَاء

bandit   a criminal who robs others, especially travelers or banks, typically using force or threat.   Outlaw, robber, thief, criminal The bandit escaped into the forest after robbing the stagecoach. لُص-قاطِع طُرُق

barbs   sharp points or projections on something, such as a fishhook or thorn. It can also mean sharp and critical remarks or comments.Jabs, taunts, criticism, spikes Her speech was filled with barbs aimed at the government's policies.   شَوْكَة

baronetcy   a hereditary title awarded in the United Kingdom, ranking below barons but above knights, often granted for services to the country or as a mark of esteem.   None directly; it is a specific title.   The baronetcy was passed down through generations in the noble family, carrying with it honor and responsibilities. البارونية

barrack   to shout loudly or jeer at someone in order to show disapproval or to encourage. Jeer, taunt, heckle, boo   The fans began to barrack the referee after a controversial decision. هَاجَمَ

barricade   a barrier or improvised obstacle set up to block or defend a place, especially during protests or emergencies. Barrier, blockade, obstacle, fortification   Protesters erected a barricade across the street to prevent police vehicles from advancing. حاجِز

barter   the exchange of goods or services for other goods or services without using money.   Trade, swap, exchange, commerce In ancient times, barter was the primary method of acquiring goods before the advent of currency.   المـَقَايِرضَـة

bayonet   a blade-like attachment that can be fixed to the muzzle of a rifle, used for stabbing or slashing in close combat. Dagger, blade, knife, weapon During the battle, soldiers fixed bayonets to their rifles for hand-to-hand combat. سكين البيونيت

beacon   a signal fire or light placed in a prominent position to guide or warn ships, aircraft, or travelers.   Signal, light, guide, marker   The lighthouse served as a beacon for ships navigating through the stormy seas. مَنارة

beadle   historically refers to a minor parish official who assists in church ceremonies and maintains order.   Church official, caretaker, usher   The beadle ensured that the church was prepared for the evening service.   كَاتِرب ُ الكَذيِسـَة

beckon   to make a gesture with the hand, arm, or head to encourage someone to come nearer or follow. Signal, gesture, summon, invite   She beckoned to her friend from across the room to join her at the table. يُشير

bedeviled   to cause great trouble or distress to someone or to be plagued or tormented by something.   Tormented, troubled, plagued, harassed   The company was bedeviled by financial problems throughout the year. مُعَذَّب

bedewing   to cover or sprinkle with dew, typically referring to something becoming wet with droplets of dew.   Drenching, wetting, moistening   The morning mist bedewed the grassy fields, creating a glistening effect under the rising sun. رَشّ النَّدى

bedridden   describes someone who is confined to bed, typically due to illness or injury, and unable to move or leave their bed.   Immobile, incapacitated, confined to bed   After the accident, he was bedridden for several weeks while recovering from his injuries. مُحدَبَّل في الفِراش

begrudging   to do something reluctantly or resentfully, often because one feels that someone does not deserve what they have been given. Resentful, jealous, envious, begrudgingly He gave her a begrudging smile after she won the competition. بِغَضَب

begrudgingly   doing something reluctantly or with ill will, often because one feels resentment or envy

towards someone else's situation.   Resentfully, grudgingly, unwillingly She begrudgingly admitted that he had done a good job, despite her initial doubts.
يِغَضَب

beguile   to charm or enchant someone in a deceptive way, often leading them to do something they might not otherwise do.   Charm, seduce, deceive, enchant   The con artist beguiled his victims with promises of quick wealth.   أغْوَى

belie   to fail to give a true idea or impression of something; to disguise or contradict the true nature of something.   Contradict, misrepresent, disguise, conceal   His calm demeanor belies the turmoil he feels inside.   يُخفّي

bellow   to shout loudly and with a deep voice, typically in anger or to attract attention.   Roar, yell, shout, holler   The coach began to bellow instructions at the players during the intense match.
يَصْرُخ

benediction   a blessing, usually given at the end of a religious service or ceremony, invoking divine help, guidance, and protection.   Blessing, invocation, prayer, consecration   The priest offered a heartfelt benediction for the newly married couple.   الصَّلاةُ-
تَبريك

benefactor   a person who gives money or other help to a person or cause, typically a charitable one.   Patron, donor, supporter, philanthropist   The library expansion was made possible by the generous donations of a local benefactor. مُحْسِن

beneficiary   a person who receives benefits or advantages, often from a will, trust, insurance policy, or other sources. Recipient, heir, inheritor, legatee   She was named as the sole beneficiary in her grandfather's will. المُستَفيد

beneficence   the quality of being kind, generous, or doing good deeds, especially towards others.   Kindness, generosity, charity, altruism   Her acts of beneficence towards the homeless shelter have greatly improved the lives of many. الإحسان

benevolence   the disposition to do good or show kindness, often demonstrated through charitable acts or goodwill towards others.   Kindness, generosity, compassion, goodwill Her acts of benevolence towards the elderly in her neighborhood brightened their days. الإحْسان

bequeath   to leave property or assets to someone by means of a will after one's death. Leave, will, hand down, bestow She chose to bequeath her antique collection to her grandchildren. وَصّى-أَوْرَث

bereave   to deprive someone of a loved one, typically by death.   Deprive, rob, take away, lose The sudden death of her husband bereaved her of her closest companion. حَرَم

bereavement   the state of mourning or grieving over the death of a loved one.   Grieving, mourning, sorrow, loss   The family struggled with their bereavement after the unexpected passing of their father. الحُزن

bereft   deprived or lacking something, especially a non-material asset like a loved one or essential quality.
Deprived, devoid, lacking, without   After losing her job, she felt bereft of purpose and direction in life.
خِذَال

berth   1. A place to sleep, typically on a ship, train, or aircraft. 2. A space allocated for a vehicle to park or dock. 3. A place or position, especially in a hierarchical organization.   1. Bed, bunk, cabin. 2. Dock, mooring, parking space. 3. Position, place, seat.   He reserved a comfortable berth on the overnight train to the city.   مَرْسَى

beseech   urgently and fervently request or implore someone for something.   Implore, beg, plead, entreat She beseeched her parents to let her go to the concert with her friends.
تَوَسَّل

beseem   to be fitting or appropriate for someone or something, especially in terms of appearance or behavior.   Befit, suit, be appropriate, befitting   His elegant attire beseemed the formal occasion perfectly.
مُلائِم

beset   1. To trouble or harass persistently. 2. To surround or attack from all sides.   1. Harass, torment, plague, trouble. 2. Surround, besiege, encircle   The company was beset by financial difficulties during the economic downturn. اجتاح

besiege   to surround a place with armed forces in order to capture it or force its surrender, or to overwhelm or beset someone with persistent requests or demands.   Surround, blockade, encircle, besiege (in the military sense); pester, harass, hound (in the figurative sense)   During the war, the army besieged the city for several months. حاصَرَ

bespoke   1. Adjective: Made to order or custom-made, especially in relation to clothing or services. 2. Past tense of bespeak: be evidence of; indicate.   1. Custom, tailored, personalized. 2. indicate, be evidence of, be a sign of, reflect, signify, denote, imply.   1. He wore a bespoke suit tailored to his exact measurements. 2. the attractive tree-lined road bespoke money.   اّلخاصّ، المُصمّم حسب الطلب-دّلالة-دل

bestir   to rouse oneself or put forth effort, typically after a period of inactivity or laziness.   Stir, rouse, motivate, energize   He finally bestirred himself to start working on his long-neglected project. يُحرّك

betide   to happen or occur, typically in a way that is unfortunate or significant.   Befall, occur, happen, transpire   She wondered what would betide her if she missed her flight. يَحْدُث

betoken   to be a sign or indication of something, typically something future or significant.   Indicate, signify, signal, presage   The dark clouds betokened an approaching storm. يُشير

betroth to enter into a formal agreement to marry someone. Engage, promise, affiance, pledge The young couple was betrothed at a traditional ceremony attended by their families. خَطَب

bickering petty arguments, usually repeated and ongoing, often about trivial matters. Quarreling, squabbling, arguing, wrangling Their constant bickering over household chores was starting to strain their relationship. مُشاحَنَة

billows can refer to large waves or surges of water, smoke, or clouds that roll or swell outward. Surge, swell, roll, wave The ship cut through the billows as it sailed across the open sea. أمواج

birch a type of tree or the wood from that tree, known for its smooth bark and often used in furniture making. Birch tree, birchwood They used birch from the forest to build their cabin. البتول

birching the act of punishing someone by beating them with a birch rod or stick, historically used as a form of corporal punishment. Whipping, flogging, caning Birching was a common form of punishment in schools during the 19th century. تَجْلِيد

bivalence refers to the state of having two possible values or conditions, typically used in logic or philosophy to describe something that can exist in two mutually exclusive states. Duality, dualism, binary nature The concept of bivalence in logic asserts that

every statement must be either true or false.
الثنائية

blatant very obvious and intentional, usually in a way that is offensive or without any attempt to hide it. Flagrant, glaring, obvious, unmistakable His blatant disregard for the rules led to his immediate expulsion from the competition. صَارِخ

boatswain (pronounced "boh-sun") is a ship's officer in charge of equipment and the crew under the direction of the ship's master. Bosun, boatswain's mate The boatswain supervised the maintenance of the ship's rigging and equipment. مَلّاح

bombastic describes speech or writing that is overly pompous or inflated, typically intended to impress others but often lacking in sincerity or meaningful content. Pompous, grandiloquent, verbose, inflatedHis bombastic speech did little to convince the audience of his sincerity. مُتَبَجِّح

bonafide (often spelled "bona fide") means genuine, real, or in good faith, especially when referring to something that is valid, sincere, or legally acceptable. Genuine, authentic, valid, legitimate She provided bonafide proof of her qualifications for the job. حَقِيقِي

boorish someone who is rough, rude, or insensitive in behavior or manners, often lacking refinement or consideration for others. Uncouth, uncivilized, rude, ill-mannered His boorish behavior at the party offended many of the guests. سَفِيه

borne   is the past participle of the verb "bear," which means to carry or support.   Carried, transported, conveyed   The burden of responsibility she had borne for years weighed heavily on her.   ذُقِل

bouts refer to short periods or spells of activity or behavior, often recurring or intermittent.   Episodes, spells, periods, sessions   He experienced bouts of creativity during late nights when everyone else was asleep. فُتُور

bower a pleasant shady place under trees or climbing plants, often used for relaxation or contemplation.   Arbor, pergola, gazebo   She loved to sit in the garden bower, surrounded by flowers and the gentle rustling of leaves.   تَعريشَة-ظَليلة-مظلّة

braggadocio empty or arrogant boasting or bravado, often to impress others.   Boasting, swaggering, arrogance, vanity   His braggadocio about his achievements quickly turned off his colleagues. مُبالَغَة-تَبَجُّح-استعراض

brandishing   to wave or exhibit something in a threatening or showy manner, especially a weapon or an object.   Waving, flourishing, displaying, showing off   He was arrested for brandishing a knife during the argument. تَهديد- إِلاَحَةّ بِهِ-أَلْمَع بـ

breeches   short trousers fastened just below the knee, worn especially in the past by men and boys.   Knickers, shorts, pants   He wore leather breeches and tall boots for the historical reenactment. سِرْوالُ قَصِير

Brevity   the quality of being concise or brief in speech or writing, using few words to convey much meaning.   Conciseness, succinctness, terseness, economy   His speech was noted for its brevity and clarity. إيجَاز

brigand   a robber or bandit, especially one who roams in a gang in wilderness areas. Bandit, outlaw, highwayman, robber   The local authorities warned travelers of the dangers posed by brigands in the mountainous region. لِص

brim   1. Noun: The upper edge or lip of a vessel or container. 2. Verb: To be full to the point of overflowing.   1. Noun: Rim, edge, lip. 2. Verb: Overflow, fill, swell.   1. The cup was filled to the brim with hot tea. 2. Her eyes brimmed with tears when she heard the news. الحَافَة-امتلأ

brio   refers to vigor, vivacity, or energy in artistic or musical performance. Vitality, vigor, energy, enthusiasm   The pianist played with great brio, captivating the audience with his lively performance. حَيَوِيَّة

brooch   a decorative piece of jewelry that is typically pinned to clothing.   Pin, badge, clasp   She wore a stunning diamond brooch on her dress for the wedding.   دبوسة

brood over   to dwell on something, typically a problem or unpleasant thought, for a prolonged period of time with a sense of worry or anxiety.   Ponder, worry about, dwell on, obsess over   She couldn't help but brood over the argument she had with her friend last night.   يَفَكَّرُ في

brusque   abrupt or blunt in manner or speech, often perceived as curt or short-tempered.   Blunt, curt, terse, abrupt   His brusque reply to her question left her feeling hurt and confused.   سَريع-جافٍ-فَظّ

buffeting   The action of striking someone or something repeatedly and violently. pounding, battering, striking   The ship withstood the buffeting of the waves during the storm.   ضرب

bugle   A brass instrument like a small trumpet, typically without valves or keys.   trumpet, horn, cornet The sound of a bugle called the soldiers to assemble.   بوق

bumptious   Irritatingly self-assertive or proud.   conceited, arrogant, self-important   The bumptious student constantly interrupted the teacher.   متغطرس

burgeoned   To begin to grow or increase rapidly; flourish.   flourished, grew, expanded   The small business burgeoned into a large corporation.   نَمَا

burgeoning   Beginning to grow or increase rapidly; flourishing.   flourishing, growing, expanding   The burgeoning population has increased the demand for housing.   نامٍ

burgher   A citizen of a town or city, typically a member of the wealthy bourgeoisie. citizen, townsman, bourgeois   The wealthy burgher lived in the largest house in the town.   مُوَاطِن

buxom   (of a woman) plump, especially with large breasts. plump, full-figured, ample   She was known for her buxom figure and cheerful personality.
ثَدِيَاء-كَاعِب-ناهِدَة

C c

caldron　　A large metal pot with a lid and handle, used for cooking over an open fire.　kettle, pot, boiler
　　The witch stirred the potion in a large, boiling caldron. غَلاَّيَة-مِرجَل

candid　Truthful and straightforward; frank.
　　Frank, honest, open, sincere, direct, forthright.
　　She was candid about her feelings towards the new project, expressing both her hopes and concerns openly. صَرِيح

candor　　The quality of being open and honest in expression; frankness.　　Frankness, openness, honesty, straightforwardness, sincerity.　　His candor during the interview impressed the hiring committee, as he openly discussed both his strengths and weaknesses. صَراحَة

caprice　　A sudden and unaccountable change of mood or behavior.　Whim, fancy, fickleness, impulsiveness, unpredictability.　　The project's direction changed on the caprice of the CEO, leaving the team scrambling to adjust. نَزْوَة

carcasses　　The dead body of an animal, especially one slaughtered and prepared for use as meat.
　　Remains, corpses, cadavers, bodies.　　The vultures circled overhead, waiting to descend upon the carcasses left in the wake of the lion's hunt. جُثَث

carnal   Relating to physical, especially sexual, needs and activities. Sexual, sensual, erotic, bodily, fleshly.
The novel explores the carnal desires of its characters, delving into the complexities of human passion.   جَسَدِيّ-شَهوَانِي

carousing   The activity of drinking alcohol and enjoying oneself with others in a noisy, lively way.
Reveling, partying, celebrating, boozing, bingeing.   The group of friends spent the night carousing at the local bar, their laughter and singing echoing through the streets.   مُعَاقَرَةُ الْخَمْر

castanet   A percussion instrument used especially in Spanish music, consisting of a pair of small concave pieces of wood, ivory, or plastic, which are clicked together by the fingers.   Clackers, clappers, bones (in context), percussion instrument. The dancer skillfully clicked the castanets in rhythm with the lively flamenco music, adding an authentic touch to the performance.   صَدَفْقَتَدَيْن-صَدَنَج

cataclysm   A large-scale and violent event in the natural world, often resulting in great destruction and change. It can also refer to any large-scale and violent upheaval, especially in a social or political context.
Disaster, Calamity, Catastrophe, Upheaval, Convulsion, Crisis   The volcanic eruption was a cataclysm that reshaped the entire region, leaving destruction in its wake.   كَارِثَة كُبْرَى

catalyst A substance that increases the rate of a chemical reaction without itself undergoing any permanent chemical change. In a broader context, it refers to a person or thing that precipitates an event or change.	Stimulus, Spark, Spur, Incitement, Motivation, Impetus	The scientist added a catalyst to the experiment to speed up the reaction, achieving results much faster than expected.	حافِز

cede	To give up power or territory, usually by treaty or agreement. It can also mean to yield or surrender something.	Surrender, Relinquish, Yield, Transfer, Give up, Concede	The country decided to cede a portion of its land to the neighboring nation in the peace agreement.	يَتَنَازَل

celibacy	The state of abstaining from marriage and sexual relations, often for religious reasons.	Abstinence, Chastity, Continence, Purity, Self-denial, Virginity	The monk took a vow of celibacy, dedicating his life entirely to spiritual pursuits.	العُزُوبَة

centripetal	Moving or tending to move toward a center. In physics, it refers to the force that acts on a body moving in a circular path and is directed toward the center around which the body is moving.	Centralizing, Unifying, Converging, Inward	The centripetal force keeps the planets in orbit around the sun, preventing them from flying off into space.	مَرْكَزِي

certitude	Absolute certainty or conviction that something is the case.	Certainty, Conviction, Confidence, Assurance, Sureness, PositivityShe spoke with such certitude about the results of the experiment that no one doubted her findings.	اليَقِين

charlatanism   The practice or behavior of a charlatan; fraudulent or deceptive behavior, particularly in claiming to have special knowledge or skills.

Deception, Fraudulence, Quackery, Trickery, Deceit, Pretending   The doctor was accused of charlatanism after it was revealed that his medical degree was fake and his treatments were ineffective.

الدَّجَّل

chastise   To rebuke or reprimand severely; to inflict punishment on. Scold, Rebuke, Reprimand, Admonish, Punish, Discipline The teacher had to chastise the student for repeatedly talking during the lecture.

يُؤَذِّب

chastity   The state or practice of refraining from extramarital, or especially from all, sexual intercourse.

Purity, Celibacy, Abstinence, Virtue, Innocence, Modesty   The vow of chastity taken by the nuns was a commitment to live a life free from sexual activity.

العِفَّة

chauvinist   A person displaying aggressive or exaggerated patriotism; a person displaying excessive or prejudiced support for their own cause, group, or sex.

Nationalist, Jingoist, Bigot, Zealot, Partisan, Sexist He was labeled a chauvinist because of his narrow-minded and biased views towards women in the workplace.

شُوفِينِي-مُتَعَصِّب

cherub   A winged angelic being described in biblical tradition as attending on God. In modern usage, it often refers to a beautiful or innocent-looking child.

Angel, Seraph, Guardian, Sprite, Heavenly being   The painting depicted a cherub with rosy cheeks and golden curls, symbolizing innocence and purity. كَرُوب-مَلاك

cherubim   Plural of cherub; winged angelic beings described in biblical tradition as attending on God and regarded in traditional Christian angelology as an order of angels.   Angels, Seraphim, Heavenly beings, Celestial beings, Guardians   The cathedral ceiling was adorned with paintings of cherubim, each one beautifully crafted to look ethereal and divine. كَرُوبِيم

chronicles   A historical account of events arranged in order of time, usually without analysis or interpretation Annals, Records, Histories, Narratives, Journals, Diaries   The ancient chronicles provide a detailed account of the kingdom's rise and fall over several centuries. السِّجِلاَّت-أَرَّخ

chuse   An archaic spelling of the word "choose," meaning to select from a number of possibilities.   Select, Pick, Opt for, Decide, Elect, Prefer   In his writings, he would often use the old-fashioned spelling "chuse" instead of "choose." يَخْتَار

ciborium   A receptacle shaped like a shrine or a cup with an arched cover, used in the Christian church to hold the consecrated Eucharistic bread.   Chalice, Vessel, Container, Receptacle, Sacred cup   The priest carefully placed the consecrated hosts into the ciborium after the Communion service. المَجْمَر

circuitously   In a way that is not straight or direct; in a roundabout manner.   Indirectly, Roundaboutly, Meanderingly, Windingly, Deviously, Tortuously
They drove circuitously through the countryside, enjoying the scenic route instead of taking the main highway.   بِطَرِيقٍ غَيْرٍ مُبَاشِرٍ

circumspect Wary and unwilling to take risks; careful to consider all circumstances and possible consequences.   Cautious, Wary, Prudent, Guarded, Careful, Vigilant   Given the sensitive nature of the situation, she was circumspect in her remarks to avoid any misunderstandings.   حَذِر

cisnormative Relating to or characterized by the assumption that being cisgender (identifying with the sex one was assigned at birth) is the norm or standard, often leading to the marginalization of non-cisgender identities.   Cis-centric, Gender-normative, Heteronormative (in related contexts), Conventional, Traditional   The organization was criticized for its cisnormative policies, which failed to acknowledge and support the needs of transgender and non-binary individuals.   سِيسْدُورمَاتِيفِي

citizenry   The citizens of a place regarded collectively; the body of citizens.   Population, Inhabitants, Residents, Society, Community, Public The government must address the concerns of the citizenry to ensure a harmonious and prosperous nation.   المُواطِنُون

clamour   A loud and confused noise, especially that of people shouting vehemently; a strong expression of public protest or demand. Outcry, Uproar, Din, Racket, Commotion, Protest The crowd's clamour for justice could be heard from miles away, as they marched through the streets demanding change. ضَجَّة

clandestine Kept secret or done secretively, especially because illicit. Secret, Covert, Hidden, Undercover, Surreptitious, Furtive The meeting was held in a clandestine location to avoid attracting attention from the authorities. سِرِّي

cleft A fissure or split, especially one in rock or the ground; a division or split in something, often referring to a physical feature. Split, Fissure, Crack, Crevice, Rift, Opening The mountain climbers carefully navigated the narrow cleft in the rock face to reach the summit. تَشَقُّق

clemency Mercy; lenience shown towards an offender or enemy. Mercy, Leniency, Compassion, Forgiveness, Pardon, Mildness The judge showed clemency by reducing the sentence of the young offender, taking into account his efforts to reform. الرَّأْفَة

clumsy Awkward in movement or handling things; lacking skill or grace. Awkward, Ungainly, Inept, Maladroit, Uncoordinated, Bungling His clumsy attempt to juggle the balls resulted in them all falling to the ground. أَخْرَق

coalesce To come together to form one mass or whole; to unite or merge for a common purpose.

Unite, Merge, Combine, Amalgamate, Fuse, Consolidate   The various community groups decided to coalesce into a single organization to have a stronger voice in local government.   يَتَحَدَّد

coalition   An alliance for combined action, especially a temporary alliance of political parties forming a government or of groups with a common interest.   Alliance, Union, Partnership, Bloc, Federation, Confederation   The coalition of environmental groups worked together to lobby for stronger conservation laws.   اِئْتِلاف

cocotte   A French term for a small casserole dish in which individual portions of food are cooked and served. It can also refer, in an archaic sense, to a flirtatious or promiscuous woman.   Casserole dish, Baking dish, Oven dish, Tart, Flirt (in the archaic sense)   She prepared a delicious ratatouille in a cocotte, serving it directly from the oven to the table. طَاجِن

coercion   The practice of persuading someone to do something by using force or threats.   Compulsion, Force, Pressure, Intimidation, Duress, Constraint   The confession was obtained through coercion, rendering it inadmissible in court.   إِكْرَاه

cog   A wheel or bar with a series of projections on its edge that transfers motion by engaging with projections on another wheel or bar. It can also refer to a person who plays a minor but necessary role in a larger organization or process.   Gear, Tooth, Sprocket, Pinion, Component, Part   In the complex machinery of the factory, each cog played a crucial role in ensuring the smooth operation of the entire system. دُرْس

cogent   Clear, logical, and convincing; compelling.   Persuasive, Compelling, Convincing, Forceful, Powerful, Logical   The lawyer's cogent argument swayed the jury, leading to a unanimous verdict in favor of her client. مُقْنِع

colicky   Relating to or suffering from colic, which is severe, often fluctuating pain in the abdomen caused by intestinal gas or obstruction in the intestines, typically affecting babies.   Crampy, Painful, Gassy, Uncomfortable, Fretful, Restless   The parents tried various remedies to soothe their colicky baby, who cried inconsolably every evening مُتَوَجِّع بِالمِغْص

colportage   The distribution of books, newspapers, and other literature, typically religious, by itinerant salespeople.   Distribution, Dissemination, Circulation, Propagation, Spread The colportage of religious texts was a crucial part of the missionary's efforts to educate and convert the local population. تَوْزِيع الكُتُب

commiserate   To express or feel sympathy or pity; to sympathize.   Sympathize, Console, Empathize, Condole, Feel for, Pity   After hearing about her friend's loss, she called to commiserate and offer her support. يُوَاسِي

committal   The act of committing a person to an institution, especially a prison or mental hospital, or the action of consigning someone to a grave.   Commitment, Consignment, Confinement,

Incarceration, Internment, Burial   The committal service was a solemn occasion, as family and friends gathered to say their final goodbyes. إِيدَاع

communal   Shared by all members of a community; for common use.   Shared, Common, Joint, Collective, Public, Cooperative   The villagers worked together to maintain the communal garden, ensuring everyone had access to fresh vegetables. مُشْتَرَك

compatible   Able to exist or work together without conflict; capable of harmonious coexistence.   Harmonious, Congruent, Consistent, Well-matched, Agreeable, Suitable   The new software is compatible with most operating systems, making it accessible to a wide range of users. مُتَوَافِق

compensatory   Intended to recompense someone who has experienced loss, suffering, or injury; serving to offset or make up for something.   Recompensatory, Redemptive, Indemnifying, Reparation, Rebalancing, Rectifying The company offered compensatory time off to employees who worked extra hours during the busy season. تَعْوِيضِي

complacent   Showing smug or uncritical satisfaction with oneself or one's achievements. Self-satisfied, Smug, Self-congratulatory, Pleased, Content, Unconcerned Despite the team's poor performance, the coach remained complacent, believing no changes were necessary.   رَاضٍ عَن ذَفْسِه

comported   Conducted oneself; behaved in a specified manner.   Behaved, Conducted, Acted, Carried, Demeaned, Managed   Despite the challenging circumstances, she comported herself with grace and dignity.   تَصَرَّف

concave   Having an outline or surface that curves inward like the interior of a circle or sphere. Hollow, Incurved, Sunken, Indented, Depressed, Recessed The mirror was concave, allowing it to focus light onto a single point.   مُقَعَّر

conceited   Excessively proud of oneself; vain and self-centered. Vain, Arrogant, Narcissistic, Self-important, Egotistical, Proud His conceited attitude made it difficult for others to work with him, as he constantly bragged about his achievements. مُتَكَبِّر

concession   The act of conceding or yielding, often a right, privilege, or point in an argument; a thing that is granted, especially in response to demands.
 Compromise, Yielding, Surrender, Grant, Allowance, Acknowledgment In the negotiations, the company made a major concession by agreeing to increase wages for the workers.   تَنَازُل

conciliatory   Intended or likely to placate or pacify; making or willing to make concessions to reconcile.
 Appeasing, Pacifying, Mollifying, Placatory, Peacemaking, Soothing   The diplomat's conciliatory approach helped to ease tensions and pave the way for peaceful negotiations. تَصَالُحِي

concoction   A mixture of various ingredients or elements, often referring to something prepared by combining different substances.   Mixture, Blend, Brew, Combination, Compound, Fusion   The chef's latest concoction was a delightful blend of exotic spices and fresh herbs.   مَزِيج

concomitant   Naturally accompanying or associated; occurring or existing concurrently.   Accompanying, Associated, Attendant, Simultaneous, Coexisting, Parallel   The rapid economic growth was accompanied by a concomitant increase in environmental pollution.   مُصَاحِب

concord   Agreement or harmony between people or groups; a treaty or covenant   Harmony, Accord, Agreement, Unity, Consensus, Peace   The two nations signed a concord to end the decades-long conflict and promote peaceful relations.   وِدَام

concordance   Agreement or harmony; an alphabetical list of the principal words used in a book or body of work, with their immediate contexts. Agreement, Harmony, Accord, Consistency, Unity, Index The concordance of the medical team's opinions was crucial in forming a unified treatment plan for the patient.   تَطَابُق

concourse   A large open space inside or in front of a public building, as in an airport or train station; a crowd or assembly of people.   Hall, Foyer, Lobby, Atrium, Gathering, Assembly The passengers waited in the bustling concourse of the train station, eagerly watching the departure board for updates.   رَدْهَة

concubine   A woman who lives with a man but has lower status than his wife or wives, often in a polygamous society.   Mistress, Paramour, Secondary wife, Courtesan, Consort   In ancient times, kings often had multiple concubines who lived in the royal palace.   سُرِّيَّة

concur   To agree or have the same opinion; to happen or occur at the same time.   Agree, Coincide, Consent, Assent, Harmonize, Accede   After much discussion, all the committee members concurred with the proposal to improve the community center.   يُتَّفِق

condescending   Having or showing a feeling of patronizing superiority.   Patronizing, Arrogant, Haughty, Supercilious, Snobbish, Lofty   Her condescending tone made it clear that she did not respect their opinions or ideas.   مِتَعَال

conducive   Making a certain situation or outcome likely or possible; contributing to a result.   Favorable, Beneficial, Helpful, Advantageous, Promoting, Supportive   The quiet environment of the library is conducive to studying and concentration   مُسَاعِد

confectionery   Sweets and chocolates considered collectively; a store that sells sweets and chocolates.   Sweets, Candy, Chocolates, Treats, Pastries, Desserts   The confectionery was filled with an array of colorful candies and decadent chocolates, tempting every customer who walked in.   الحَلْوَيَات

confinement The state of being confined or restricted within certain limits or boundaries; imprisonment.
Imprisonment, Incarceration, Detention, Restriction, Custody, Captivity   The prisoner endured years of confinement in a small cell, isolated from the outside world.   الدَبْس

conformity   Compliance with standards, rules, or laws; behavior in accordance with socially accepted conventions or standards.   Compliance, Adherence, Obedience, Accordance, Agreement, Alignment   The school's dress code ensures that all students maintain a level of conformity in their appearance.   الإِنْصِريَاع

confounded Used for emphasis, especially to express anger or annoyance; confused or perplexed.Bewildered, Perplexed, Baffled, Mystified, Puzzled, Stumped   He was confounded by the complex instructions, unable to figure out how to assemble the furniture.   مُرْتَبِك

congeal   To solidify or coagulate, especially by cooling; to take shape or become fixed in a particular form.   Solidify, Coagulate, Harden, Thicken, Set, Clot   As the temperature dropped, the liquid in the container began to congeal into a gel-like substance.   يَتَجَمَّد

conival   Related to or resembling a cone; having a cone-like shape.   Conic, Conical, Cone-shaped, Tapered, Pyramidal, Pointed   The conival hills in the region create a unique and striking landscape that attracts many tourists.   مَخْرُوطِي

connivance   Willingness to secretly allow or be involved in wrongdoing, especially an immoral or illegal act.   Collusion, Complicity, Consent, Collaboration, Participation, Conspiracy   The manager's connivance in the fraud led to his eventual dismissal and criminal charges. تَوَاطُؤ

connoisseur   An expert judge in matters of taste, especially in the fine arts, food, or drink.   Expert, Aficionado, Specialist, Authority, Savant, Gourmet   As a connoisseur of fine wines, she could identify the region and vintage of a wine with just one sip.   خَبِير

connubiality   The state of being married; marital relations.   Matrimony, Marriage, Wedlock, Spousal relationship, Conjugality, Marital union   Their connubiality was evident in the way they supported and cared for each other through thick and thin. حَالَة الزَّوَاج

consolidation   The action or process of making something stronger or more solid; the process of combining a number of things into a single more effective or coherent whole.   Unification, Integration, Amalgamation, Strengthening, Merging, Combination   The company focused on the consolidation of its various departments to improve efficiency and reduce costs. تَعْزِيز

consumptive   Relating to or affected with a wasting disease, especially pulmonary tuberculosis. Tubercular, Wasting, Emaciated, Debilitated, Cachectic, Diseased   In the 19th century, many people succumbed to consumptive illnesses due to the lack of effective medical treatments.   مُصَاب بِالسُّلّ

contending   Engaging in a competition or struggle; asserting something as a position in an argument.

Competing, Struggling, Fighting, Asserting, Arguing, Disputing   Several teams were contending for the championship title, each displaying remarkable skill and determination.   يَتَدَافَس

contested   Disputed or challenged, often in the context of a competition, election, or argument.

Disputed, Challenged, Contended, Opposed, Argued, Debated   The results of the election were hotly contested, leading to a recount and further scrutiny of the voting process.   مُتَدَازَع عَلَيْه

contingent   Dependent on something else that might or might not happen; a group of people united by some common feature, forming part of a larger group.

Dependent, Conditional, Subject to, Possible, Provisional, Probable The success of the project is contingent upon securing sufficient funding from investors.   مُعْتَمِد عَلَى

contrite   Feeling or expressing remorse or penitence; affected by guilt.   Remorseful, Repentant, Penitent, Apologetic, Regretful, Rueful   She was genuinely contrite for her actions and sought to make amends with those she had wronged.   نَادِم

contrive   To create or bring about (an object or a situation) by deliberate use of skill and artifice.

Devise, Engineer, Fabricate, Plan, Scheme, Manipulate   The spy managed to contrive an elaborate plan to escape from the heavily guarded facility. يَخْتَرِع

convalesce   To recover one's health and strength over a period of time after an illness or medical treatment.   Recuperate, Recover, Heal, Mend, Improve, Revitalize   After the surgery, she needed several weeks to convalesce before she could return to her regular activities. يَتَعَافَى

convex   Having a surface or outline that curves outward like the exterior of a sphere or circle.   Bulging, Curved, Rounded, Arched, Protruding, Swollen   The convex lens helped to magnify the small print, making it easier to read. مُحَدَّب

convolute   To make (something) complex and difficult to follow; to coil up or twist.   Complicate, Twist, Entangle, Confound, Wind, Spiral   The author tended to convolute his narratives, making them challenging for readers to follow. يُعَقِّد

convoluted   Extremely complex and difficult to follow; intricately folded, twisted, or coiled.   Complicated, Intricate, Complex, Tangled, Elaborate, Confusing   The professor's explanation of the theory was so convoluted that most of the students were left utterly confused. مُتَعَرِّج

copious   Abundant in supply or quantity.   Abundant, Plentiful, Ample, Profuse, Lavish, Generous   The students took copious notes during the lecture to ensure they didn't miss any important information. وَافِر

coquettish　　Behaving in a flirtatious way. Flirtatious, Teasing, Playful, Provocative, Seductive, Coy　　She gave him a coquettish smile, hinting at her interest without saying a word. غَزِلَة

corduroy　　A thick cotton fabric with velvety ribs. Ribbed fabric, Ribbed cotton, Pile fabric　　He wore a pair of brown corduroy pants that were both stylish and warm. قُطْن مُضَلَّع

cornucopia　　A symbol of plenty consisting of a goat's horn overflowing with flowers, fruit, and corn; an abundant supply of good things.　　Abundance, Profusion, Plentifulness, Wealth, Overflow, Bounty　The harvest festival featured a cornucopia of fresh fruits, vegetables, and homemade goods. قَرْنُ ٱلثَّرْوَة

correctitude　　The quality of being correct or proper in conduct or belief; correctness.　　Correctness, Appropriateness, Propriety, Rectitude, Properness, Decency　　His strict adherence to social norms and correctitude made him a model citizen in the eyes of his community.　صِحَّة

corroborating　　　Providing evidence or information that supports or confirms a statement, theory, or finding.　　Confirming, Supporting, Validating, Verifying, Substantiating, Upholding　　The witness's testimony was crucial in corroborating the defendant's alibi, leading to an acquittal. يُؤَيِّد

corrode　　to gradually wear away, typically by chemical action. This process usually involves metals

deteriorating due to reactions with their environment.
Erode, rust, decay, tarnish, deteriorate, oxidize
If left exposed to the elements, the metal will
begin to corrode, eventually weakening the structure.
تَآكَل

corrosive   refers to a substance that has the ability
to cause damage or destruction to materials, especially
metals, through a chemical reaction. Caustic, erosive,
abrasive, destructive, damaging, oxidizing   The factory
had to implement special safety measures to handle the
corrosive chemicals used in production.   مُتَآكِل

corrugated   a material shaped into alternating ridges
and grooves, often used to add strength and rigidity.
Ribbed, fluted, grooved, furrowed, wavy, ridged
The roofing was made of corrugated metal
sheets to ensure durability and resistance against harsh
weather conditions.   مُمَوَّج

counterintuitive   describes something that goes
against what one would intuitively expect or believe.
Unexpected, illogical, paradoxical, surprising,
contrary, implausible It may seem counterintuitive, but
drinking more water can actually help reduce water
retention in the body. مُخَالِف لِلْبَدِيهِيَّة

coup   a sudden, decisive, and often illegal overthrow
of a government or leadership, usually carried out by a
small group.   Overthrow, takeover, rebellion,
insurrection, mutiny, revolution   The military coup
resulted in the swift removal of the country's
democratically elected leader.   اِنْقِلَاب

courting   the process of seeking the affection or favor of someone, often with the intention of forming a romantic relationship or marriage.   Wooing, dating, pursuing, romancing, charming, suiting   They spent several months courting before he finally proposed to her.   مُغَازَلَة

credence   belief in or acceptance of something as true.   Belief, faith, trust, confidence, reliance, acceptance   The witness's testimony gave credence to the defendant's alibi, leading to his acquittal.
مَصْدَاقِيَّة

credo a statement of the beliefs or aims that guide someone's actions.   Creed, doctrine, philosophy, tenet, principle, ideology   The company's credo emphasizes sustainability and social responsibility in all its business practices. عَقِيدَة

credulous   someone who is too ready to believe things and therefore easily fooled or deceived.
Gullible, naive, trusting, unsuspecting, innocent, unquestioning The scam artist targeted credulous individuals who were quick to believe his false promises of instant wealth.   سَاذِج

crevice   a narrow opening or fissure, especially in a rock or wall. Crack, fissure, gap, chasm, split, cleft
The hiker found a small crevice in the rock where he could take shelter from the storm.   شَقّ

crooning   singing in a soft, low, and intimate manner, often with a sentimental tone.   Singing softly, murmuring, serenading, humming, warbling,

chanting   The singer captivated the audience by crooning a beautiful love song, leaving everyone in awe of his voice.   تَغْنِيَةٌ بِلَحْنٍ عَذْب

crudity   the quality of being rudimentary, raw, or lacking in refinement and sophistication.   Coarseness, roughness, rawness, crudeness, primitiveness, vulgarity   Despite the crudity of his early sketches, the artist's talent was evident and eventually blossomed into a refined style.   بَذَاءَة-خَامِيَّة-فَظَاظَة

culminate   to reach the highest point, climax, or final stage of something.   Peak, climax, conclude, finish, reach, terminate   The months of hard work and preparation will culminate in the company's grand product launch next week.   يَبْلُغُ ذُرْوَتَه

culpability   refers to the responsibility for a fault or wrong; blame. Blame, fault, guilt, responsibility, accountability, liability The investigation aimed to determine the culpability of the various parties involved in the financial scandal.   مَسْؤُولِيَّة

culpable   describes being deserving of blame or considered responsible for a wrongdoing.   Guilty, blameworthy, at fault, responsible, answerable, liable   The jury found the defendant culpable for the crime, leading to his conviction.   مُسْتَحِقّ لِلَّوْم

culprit   a person who is responsible for a crime or other misdeed.   Offender, wrongdoer, perpetrator, criminal, transgressor, malefactor   After a thorough investigation, the police finally caught the culprit who had been vandalizing the neighborhood.   مُتَّهَم

cumbersome   something that is large, heavy, and difficult to carry or use; unwieldy.   Unwieldy, clumsy, bulky, awkward, heavy, inconvenient The movers struggled with the cumbersome sofa as they tried to fit it through the narrow doorway. ثَقيلُ الوَزْن

curb   to restrain or keep in check. Restrain, control, limit, check, restrict, rein in   The government implemented new policies to curb inflation and stabilize the economy. يُحَدُّد

cutlet   a small, boneless piece of meat, often breaded and fried, or a similar vegetarian dish made with a substitute like vegetables or legumes.   Chop, fillet, steak, patty, escalope For dinner, we enjoyed delicious chicken cutlets served with a side of mashed potatoes and steamed vegetables.   شَريحَة لَحْم

D d

dallied   1. to waste time or act slowly. 2. to engage in a casual romantic or sexual relationship.   Loitered, lingered, dawdled, tarried, delayed, procrastinated, trifle, toy, flirt, philander, womenize   1. He dallied on his way to work, stopping at several coffee shops and taking his time to enjoy the morning. 2. he should stop dallying with film stars.   تَمَاهَل-غَازَل

dalmatic   a long, wide-sleeved tunic, worn by deacons and bishops in some Christian liturgical traditions.   Tunic, robe, vestment, garment, surplice   During the solemn ceremony, the deacon wore a beautifully embroidered dalmatic that symbolized his role in the service.   دَلْمَاتِيقَة

de-emphasize   to reduce the importance or prominence given to something.   Downplay, minimize, understate, lessen, diminish, marginalize In his presentation, he chose to de-emphasize the company's past mistakes and focus on their recent successes.   يُقَلِّل مِنْ أَهَمِّيَّة

deacon   a member of the clerical order just below a priest in the hierarchy of the Christian church, often involved in various ministries and services. Cleric, minister, ecclesiastic, church officer, servant, attendant   The deacon delivered a moving sermon that resonated deeply with the congregation.   شَمَّاس

debase   to reduce in quality, value, or dignity; to degrade.   Degrade, demean, lower, tarnish, corrupt, diminish   The scandal served to debase the reputation of the once-respected politician. يُحَطِّمُ مِنْ قِيمَة

debasing   the act of reducing in quality, value, or dignity; degrading.   Degrading, demeaning, lowering, tarnishing, corrupting, diminishing   The constant spread of misinformation is debasing the quality of public discourse. تَحْطِيمُ القِيمَة

debauch   to corrupt morally or to lead someone away from virtue or excellence, often through excessive indulgence in sensual pleasures.   Corrupt, degrade, defile, pervert, seduce, lead astray   The once-promising student was debauched by the temptations of a reckless lifestyle, abandoning his studies and ambitions. يُفْسِدُ أَخْلاَق

debilitated   weakened or incapacitated, often due to illness, injury, or other adverse conditions.   Weakened, enfeebled, incapacitated, impaired, exhausted, frail   After the long illness, he was debilitated and needed several weeks to regain his strength. مُوهَن

debilitating   causing severe weakness or incapacitation, making someone very weak or unable to function effectively.   Weakening, enfeebling, exhausting, incapacitating, crippling, paralyzing   The debilitating effects of the disease left him unable to perform even the simplest daily tasks without assistance. مُوهِن

debris   scattered fragments, typically of something wrecked or destroyed; rubble or waste.   Rubble, wreckage, remains, fragments, litter, detritus   After the storm passed, the streets were filled with debris from fallen trees and damaged buildings.   حُطَام

decanter   a vessel, typically glass or crystal, used for holding and serving wine or other liquids, often designed to allow the liquid to breathe.   Carafe, vessel, jug, bottle, flask, container   The host poured the vintage wine into a beautiful crystal decanter before serving it to the guests.   قَارُورَة

decimated   to destroy a large proportion of something, often used to describe severe damage or destruction.   Devastated, destroyed, annihilated, obliterated, ravaged, reduced   The small village was decimated by the hurricane, leaving few buildings standing.   مُدَمَّر

declivity   a downward slope or bend.   Slope, descent, decline, gradient, inclination, dip   Hiking up the steep inclines was challenging, but the gentle declivity on the way down made for an easier return.   مُنْحَدَر

decorum   behavior that is well-mannered, polite, and in keeping with accepted standards of propriety.   Etiquette, propriety, manners, politeness, courtesy, dignity   The queen's unwavering sense of decorum was evident in every public appearance, setting a standard for the entire royal family. لِيَاقَة

decrepit describes something that is worn out or ruined because of age or neglect. Dilapidated, ramshackle, rickety, broken-down, aged, frail The decrepit house on the corner had been abandoned for years, with its roof caving in and windows shattered. مُتَهَدِّم

defamatory something that is damaging to someone's reputation through false or unjust statements. Slanderous, libelous, injurious, disparaging, harmful, maligning The journalist was sued for writing a defamatory article that falsely accused the politician of corruption. تَشْهيري

defective something that is imperfect or faulty, having a flaw or fault. Faulty, flawed, imperfect, malfunctioning, broken, deficient The company had to recall the defective products after numerous complaints from customers about their malfunction. مُعَاب

defiance a bold resistance to authority or an opposing force; open disobedience or disregard. Resistance, rebellion, disobedience, insubordination, opposition, noncompliance In a show of defiance, the protesters refused to leave the streets despite the government's orders. تَحَدِّ

degloving a severe injury where a large section of skin and the underlying tissue is torn off from the hand or another part of the body, often resembling the removal of a glove. Skin avulsion, traumatic avulsion, severe skin tear, tissue stripping The accident resulted in a degloving injury to the cyclist's arm,

requiring immediate and extensive medical treatment.
إِزَالَةُ الجِلْد

deification   the act of worshiping, revering, or elevating someone or something to the status of a god.
Apotheosis, glorification, exaltation, idolization, divinization, veneration   The ancient pharaohs sought deification, often being worshiped as gods by their people.   تَأْلِيه

deign   to do something that one considers beneath one's dignity; to condescend to give or grant.
Condescend, stoop, lower oneself, consent, agree, patronize   She did not deign to reply to the rude comment, considering it unworthy of her attention.
يَتَفَضَّل

dejection   a state of sadness, depression, or low spirits. Depression, despondency, sadness, gloom, melancholy, discouragement After receiving the rejection letter from her dream job, she felt a deep sense of dejection and hopelessness.   اِكْتِئَاب

delectation   to pleasure and delight.   Enjoyment, pleasure, delight, gratification, amusement, satisfaction
The gourmet meal was prepared with such skill and creativity that it was a true delectation for the senses.   مُتْعَة

delicatessen   a shop that sells high-quality, ready-to-eat foods, such as cooked meats, cheeses, salads, and specialty items.   Deli, gourmet food shop, charcuterie, fine foods store   We stopped by the local delicatessen to pick up some fresh sandwiches and imported cheeses for the picnic. مَحَلّ بَيْعِ الأَطْعِمَةِ الفَاخِرَةِ

delineation   the act of describing or portraying something precisely, or the act of outlining or marking the boundary of something.   Description, depiction, portrayal, outline, representation, definition   The architect provided a clear delineation of the new building's layout, ensuring everyone understood the design. تَحْدِيد

delinquent   someone, typically a young person, who has a tendency to commit minor crimes or misbehave; it can also refer to something that is overdue or neglected, such as a payment.   Offender, wrongdoer, criminal, miscreant, lawbreaker, defaulter   The teenager was labeled a delinquent after repeatedly skipping school and getting into trouble with the law.   مُخَالِف

delirious   a disturbed state of mind resulting from illness or intoxication, characterized by restlessness, illusions, and incoherence; extremely excited or enthusiastic.   Hysterical, incoherent, raving, feverish, ecstatic, frenzied   After the long and exhausting journey, he became delirious, speaking in incoherent sentences and seeing things that weren't there.   هَاذٍ

deluded   believing something that is not true, often as a result of being deceived or having a false impression.   Deceived, misled, fooled, tricked, mistaken, duped   He was deluded into thinking he could achieve success without hard work and dedication.   مُوْهَم

delve   to investigate or research deeply into a subject or topic.   Investigate, explore, examine, research, probe, dig into She decided to delve into the history of her family, uncovering fascinating stories about her ancestors.   يَتَعَمَّقُ في

demagogic   refers to the practices of a demagogue, which involve appealing to emotions, fears, prejudices, or ignorance of the public to gain power and manipulate people, often through false promises and inflammatory rhetoric.   Agitative, incendiary, inflammatory, rabble-rousing, populist, manipulative   The politician's demagogic speeches stirred up fear and anger among the populace, leading to increased division and unrest.   تَحْرِيضِي

demagogue   a political leader who seeks support by appealing to popular desires, emotions, fears, and prejudices rather than by using rational argument.   Agitator, rabble-rouser, firebrand, provocateur, manipulator, populist The demagogue gained a massive following by promising simple solutions to complex problems and blaming societal issues on a specific group.   زَعِيم شَعْبَوِي

demiurge   a being responsible for the creation of the universe, particularly in Platonic and Gnostic philosophy; it can also refer to a powerful creative force or a guiding principle. Creator, architect, maker, artisan, deity, craftsman   In Gnostic belief, the demiurge is considered a lesser god who created the material world, often seen as imperfect or flawed.   الخَالِق, الصَّانِع

demoted   to be reduced to a lower rank, grade, or position.   Downgraded, degraded, reduced, lowered, displaced, deposed After failing to meet the company's performance standards, he was demoted from manager to assistant manager. مُنَزَّلُ الرُّتْبَة

demotion   the act of reducing someone to a lower rank or position, often as a form of punishment or due to performance issues. Downgrading, degradation, relegation, reduction, **deposition**   After the series of critical errors in the project, John faced a demotion from his managerial role to a regular team member.
اِلتَّخْفِيضُ فِي الرُّتْبَة

denizen   an inhabitant or occupant of a particular place. Inhabitant, resident, dweller, occupant, native
The denizen of the small village was known for his extensive knowledge of local folklore and traditions.
مُقِيم

denomination   a term used to describe a recognized autonomous branch of the Christian Church, a unit of value (like currency), or a name or designation, especially one serving to classify a set of things.
Sect, branch, division, group, unit, category
Each denomination of the currency is easily distinguishable by its unique color and size. تَسْمِيَة

denouncement   the public condemnation or criticism of someone or something, often in a formal manner.   Condemnation, censure, criticism, accusation, rebuke   The leader's denouncement of corruption within the government was widely covered by the media.   إِدَانَة

deplorable   describes something deserving strong condemnation, shockingly bad in quality, or causing grief or regret. Disgraceful, lamentable, appalling, wretched, reprehensible   The living conditions in the abandoned building were absolutely deplorable, with no running water or electricity. مُؤَسِرّف

deplore   to feel or express strong disapproval of something, or to regret deeply.   Condemn, lament, denounce, regret, bewail   The community leaders deplore the recent acts of violence and are calling for peace and unity. يُشْجُب

depose   to remove someone from office or power, typically in a formal or forceful manner, or to testify or give evidence under oath, usually in a written statement.   Remove, overthrow, unseat, dethrone, testify The military coup aimed to depose the corrupt dictator and restore democratic governance.يَعْزِل

depravity   moral corruption or wickedness.   Corruption, immorality, wickedness, vice, debauchery   The novel's villain was a character of extreme depravity, delighting in the suffering of others. فَسَاد

deprecatory   describes a manner or expression that shows disapproval, criticism, or belittlement.   Disapproving, critical, belittling, disparaging, derogatory   She gave a deprecatory glance at his messy handwriting, clearly unimpressed by his lack of effort. تَثْبِيطِيّ-اِستهجاني

derisive something that expresses ridicule or mockery. Mocking, scornful, contemptuous, taunting, sneering His derisive laughter at her suggestion made it clear that he had no respect for her ideas. اِسْتِهْزَائِي

derogatory describes something that shows a critical or disrespectful attitude. Disparaging, belittling, demeaning, insulting, defamatory The employee was fired for making derogatory comments about his coworkers. تَحْقِيرِي

desensitization the process of making someone less sensitive to something, typically through repeated exposure. Numbing, habituation, acclimatization, inurement, immunization Constant exposure to violent video games can lead to the desensitization of young players to real-world violence. إِزَالَةُ التَّحَسُّس

desideratum something that is needed or wanted. Requirement, necessity, essential, need, want The main desideratum for the project to succeed is sufficient funding and skilled personnel. مَطْلُوبٌ- رَغِيبَة

desirous describes having or expressing a strong wish or desire for something. Eager, longing, yearning, craving, wanting She was desirous of a promotion, working extra hours and taking on additional responsibilities to prove her worth. مُشْتَهِ

desist means to cease or abstain from an action. Cease, stop, refrain, quit, haltThe judge ordered the company to desist from using the controversial advertisement. يُكَفُّ

desolation   a state of complete emptiness or destruction, or extreme sadness and loneliness.   Devastation, ruin, bleakness, barrenness, loneliness   After the war, the once vibrant city was left in utter desolation, with buildings reduced to rubble and streets eerily silent. كَآبَة

despondence   a state of low spirits caused by loss of hope or courage.   Despair, dejection, hopelessness, gloom, melancholy   After several failed attempts to find a job, he fell into a state of despondence, feeling that his efforts were in vain. اِكْتِئَاب

despondency   a state of low spirits caused by loss of hope or courage.   Despair, dejection, hopelessness, gloom, melancholy   After several failed attempts to find a job, he fell into a state of despondency, feeling that his efforts were in vain. يَأْس

despondent   a feeling or showing of hopelessness, dejection, or being in low spirits.   Disheartened, discouraged, downcast, dejected, hopeless After hearing the bad news, she felt despondent and couldn't find the energy to continue her work. مُحْبَط

despotism   the exercise of absolute power, especially in a cruel and oppressive way.   Tyranny, dictatorship, autocracy, totalitarianism, authoritarianism   The citizens revolted against the despotism of the ruling regime, demanding democracy and human rights. اِسْتِبْدَاد

detriment	the state of being harmed or damaged, or something that causes harm or damage. Harm, damage, injury, disadvantage, loss Excessive screen time can be to the detriment of a child's eyesight and overall health. ضَرَر

deucedly	an informal British adverb meaning very or extremely. Very, extremely, exceedingly, terribly, exceptionally He found the puzzle deucedly difficult and spent hours trying to solve it.	بِشَكْلٍ كَبِير

devilment	reckless or mischievous behavior, often causing trouble or annoyance.	Mischief, naughtiness, prankishness, roguery, troublemaking The children's constant devilment kept their parents on edge throughout the entire trip.	شَغَب

diadem	a jeweled crown or headband worn as a symbol of sovereignty.	Crown, coronet, tiara, circlet, chaplet The queen's diadem sparkled brilliantly under the lights, symbolizing her royal authority.	تَاج

dialectic	the art of investigating or discussing the truth of opinions, often through logical argumentation or the juxtaposition of contradictory ideas to find a synthesis.	Logic, reasoning, debate, discussion, argumentation The philosopher's dialectic method involved questioning and refuting his students' ideas to help them reach a deeper understanding of the subject. جَدَل

diaspora   the dispersion or spread of any people from their original homeland. Displacement, dispersion, scattering, migration, exodus The Jewish diaspora has a long history, with communities established all over the world. شَتَتَات

diffident   someone who is modest or shy due to a lack of self-confidence.   Shy, timid, reserved, self-conscious, unassertive   Despite her diffident nature, she managed to deliver an impressive presentation to the board of directors. خَجُول

diffidence   modesty or shyness resulting from a lack of self-confidence.   Shyness, timidity, modesty, self-doubt, insecurity   His diffidence prevented him from speaking up during the meeting, even though he had valuable ideas to share. خَجَل

dignitaries   people who hold high rank or office, often in the government or a significant organization. Officials, luminaries, VIPs, notables, authorities The event was attended by various dignitaries, including ambassadors, ministers, and prominent business leaders. الشَّخْصِيَّاتُ الْمَرْمُوقَة

dilapidated   describes something that is in a state of disrepair or ruin due to age or neglect.   Ruined, decayed, decrepit, ramshackle, shabby   The old mansion, once grand and elegant, now stood dilapidated, with broken windows and a collapsing roof. مُتَهَدِّم

dilated   made wider or larger; expanded. Expanded, enlarged, widened, stretched, spread   The doctor examined her dilated pupils to check for any neurological issues. مُتَوَسِّع

dilettante   a person who takes up an art, activity, or subject merely for amusement, especially in a superficial way; a dabbler.   Amateur, dabbler, novice, nonprofessional, layperson   While he enjoyed painting as a hobby, his approach was that of a dilettante, never delving deeply into the techniques or history of the art. مُتَهَاوِن-غاوِي-هُوَاتي

diligence   careful and persistent work or effort.   Industriousness, perseverance, assiduity, conscientiousness, meticulousness   Her diligence in studying every day paid off when she achieved the highest marks in her class.   اِجْتِهَاد

diminutive   something that is extremely or unusually small.   Tiny, small, petite, miniature, little   The diminutive puppy could fit comfortably in the palm of your hand.   صَغِير جِدّاً

dirge   a lament for the dead, especially one forming part of a funeral rite or any mournful song or piece of music. Lament, elegy, requiem, funeral song, threnody   The mourners sang a solemn dirge as they carried the casket to the grave.   رِثَاء

disavow   to deny any responsibility for or connection with something.   Deny, repudiate, disclaim, renounce, reject   The politician was quick to disavow any knowledge of the scandal that had shaken the government.   يَتَبَرَّأ

Discern perceive or recognize something, often with difficulty. Detect, perceive, recognize, notice, distinguish Even in the dim light, she could discern the outline of the mountains in the distance. يُمَيِّز

discombobulating describes something that causes confusion or disorientation. Confusing, bewildering, perplexing, unsettling, baffling The rapid changes in the schedule were discombobulating for the new employees, who struggled to keep up. مُرْبِك

discord a lack of harmony or agreement, often leading to conflict. Conflict, disagreement, strife, dissonance, friction The discord between the two departments hindered the progress of the entire project. خِلاَف-خُصُومَة-فِتْنَة

discretion the quality of behaving or speaking in such a way as to avoid causing offense or revealing confidential information, or the freedom to decide what should be done in a particular situation. Prudence, judgment, circumspection, caution, tact The manager handled the sensitive issue with great discretion, ensuring that no one was unnecessarily embarrassed. تَحَفُّظ

Disdain the feeling that someone or something is unworthy of one's consideration or respect; contempt. Contempt, scorn, derision, disparagement, condescension She looked at the messy room with disdain, unable to comprehend how anyone could live in such chaos. ازْدِرَاء

disheveled   describes someone or something that is untidy, messy, or in disorder. Untidy, messy, unkempt, disordered, tousled   After a long day of work, his hair was disheveled and his clothes were wrinkled. مُشَعْثَر

dispense   1. to distribute or provide (a service or information) to a number of people. 2. to manage without; get rid of.   1. Distribute, allocate, issue, supply, provide. 2. omit, drop, forgo, relinquish   1. The pharmacist is authorized to dispense medications to patients with a valid prescription. 2. let's dispense with the formalities, shall we? يُوَزِّع-اِسْتَغْنَى عن

disquisition   a long or elaborate essay or discussion on a particular subject.   Treatise, essay, dissertation, discourse, analysis   The professor's disquisition on ancient philosophy captivated the entire class with its depth and insight. بَحْث مُسْتَفِيض

disseminate   to spread or disperse (something, especially information) widely.   Distribute, spread, circulate, propagate, broadcast   The organization aims to disseminate knowledge about sustainable practices to communities around the world. يَنْشُر

dissemination   the act of spreading something, especially information, widely.   Distribution, spread, circulation, propagation, broadcasting   The dissemination of accurate information is crucial during a public health crisis to prevent misinformation. نَشْر

Dissent   the expression or holding of opinions that are different from those previously, commonly, or officially expressed.   Disagreement, opposition, protest, discord, conflict   The new policy was met with widespread dissent from employees who felt it was unfair and impractical.مُعارَضَة

dissenter   a person who dissents, especially one who disagrees with the majority opinion, belief, or policies.   Opponent, objector, protester, dissident, critic   The dissenter argued passionately against the proposed changes during the meeting, highlighting their potential negative impact.   مُعَارِض

disservice   an action that harms or damages someone or something, often by not fulfilling one's duty or responsibility.   Harm, injury, damage, detriment, disadvantage It would be a disservice to the community to close down the local library, as it serves as a vital resource for many residents. ضَرَر

dissident   a person who actively opposes official policy, especially that of an authoritarian state.   Rebel, protester, dissenter, opponent, critic The dissident was arrested for organizing protests against government corruption.   مُعَارِض

dissipation   1. The process of squandering or wasting resources, especially time or money, in a reckless or extravagant manner. 2. The dispersion or dissolving of something, typically energy or heat.   1. Squandering, waste, extravagance, excess. 2. Dispersion, dissolving, dispersal, scattering. 1. His life was marked by dissipation, spending his inheritance on parties and luxury. 2. The dissipation of heat from the engine was causing it to overheat.   التَّبَذُّر-التَّشَتُّت

dissolution   1. The act or process of ending something, such as a marriage, partnership, or organization. 2. The breaking up or dispersion of something into smaller parts. 3. The process of dissolving a substance in a solvent.   1. Termination, breakup, separation, disintegration. 2. Dispersal, scattering, disbandment, fragmentation. 3. Dissolving, melting, liquefaction, dilution. 1. The dissolution of their business partnership was amicable, with both parties agreeing to part ways. 2. The dissolution of the sugar in water created a sweet solution. 3. The dissolution of the empire led to various smaller kingdoms emerging in its place. التَّحْلِيف-التَّفَكُّك-الذَّوَابَة

dissuade   to persuade someone not to take a particular course of action.   Deter, discourage, advise against, talk out of, counsel against She tried to dissuade him from quitting his job without having another lined up, emphasizing the risks involved.   يُثْنِي

ditty   a short, simple song or tune, typically with words that are easy to remember.   Song, tune, melody, jingle, chant   He hummed a cheerful ditty as he worked in the garden, brightening up his afternoon. "أُغْنِيَة" قَصِيرَة

divisive   something that causes disagreement or discord among people, creating division or hostility.   Controversial, polarizing, contentious, discordant, antagonistic   The issue of immigration reform proved to be highly divisive, splitting public opinion sharply. مُثَيِّر للفِرْقَة

divulge   to make known (private or sensitive information) to others. Reveal, disclose, expose, impart, leak   She refused to divulge the source of her information, fearing repercussions from her colleagues. يُفْشِي

doctrinaire   describes someone who rigidly adheres to a set of beliefs or principles, often without regard to practical considerations or differing opinions.
     Dogmatic, rigid, inflexible, uncompromising, authoritarian   His doctrinaire approach to management often clashed with the flexible and adaptive strategies preferred by his team. عُقْدِيّ

dogmatic   someone who asserts opinions or beliefs as if they are indisputably true, often without considering other viewpoints. Opinionated, doctrinaire, inflexible, rigid, authoritarian   She was known for her dogmatic insistence on following the rules exactly as written, even when flexibility could have led to a better outcome.   عُقْدِي

dole   1. As a noun, it refers to a small portion or share of something, especially money or food, given out to someone in need. 2. As a verb, it means to distribute shares of something, usually money or food, to those in need.   1. (Noun) Allowance, allocation, portion, share, grant. 2. (Verb) Distribute, allocate, dispense, give out, hand out.   1. The government provides a monthly dole to unemployed citizens to help them meet their basic needs. 2. Volunteers dole out food and clothing to homeless individuals every Saturday in the park.
     مَعْوَنَة-يُوزِّع

doleful   something that is mournful or expressing sorrow; filled with or evoking sadness.
        Sorrowful, mournful, melancholy, sad, woeful
        The doleful music played softly in the background during the memorial service, adding to the solemn atmosphere. مُحْزِن

dolorous   describes something that is full of or expressing sorrow or pain.   Sorrowful, mournful, grievous, plaintive, melancholy   The dolorous cries of the grieving widow echoed through the empty hallways of the mansion.   مُحْزِن

domineering   someone who asserts their will over others in an arrogant or overbearing manner, often disregarding their opinions or feelings.
        Authoritarian, dictatorial, bossy, controlling, overbearing   Her domineering attitude in the workplace alienated many of her colleagues, who felt their input was constantly disregarded.   مُتَسَلِّط

don   as a verb means to put on or dress oneself in a particular item of clothing.   Wear, put on, dress in, attire oneself in   He donned his coat and hat before heading out into the cold winter night.
    ارْتَدَى

dovetail   1. Noun: A joint formed by one or more tapered projections (tenons) on one piece that interlock with corresponding notches or recesses (mortises) in another piece, used especially in woodworking. 2. Verb: To fit together harmoniously, like the fitting of dovetail joints. 1. Noun: Joint, interlocking joint, mortise and tenon joint. 2. Verb: Fit together, mesh, complement,

interlock.   1. The skilled carpenter crafted the drawers with dovetail joints for added strength and durability. 2. Their skills and interests dovetailed perfectly, making them a formidable team.
المفصل العمودي-تَدَلاَمَس

draconian   refers to laws, measures, or actions that are extremely harsh, severe, or strict.   Harsh, severe, stringent, rigorous, oppressive   The government's response to the protest was criticized as draconian, with heavy fines and arrests of peaceful demonstrators.   قَاسٍ لِلْغَايَة

droplet   a very small drop of a liquid.   Drop, bead, particle, speck   After the rain, small droplets of water clung to the leaves of the trees.   قَطْرَة

drudgery   hard, menial, or dull work, especially when it is repetitive or monotonous. Toil, labor, grind, slog, chore   She endured years of drudgery in the factory before finally saving enough money to start her own business. مَهِنَة مُسْتَنْقِرَة

dubious   describes something that is uncertain, questionable, or doubtful, often implying suspicion or mistrust.   Questionable, uncertain, suspicious, doubtful, skeptical   His dubious explanation for arriving late did little to reassure his boss about his commitment to the project.   مُشَكَك

dud   1. Noun: An object, especially a weapon or explosive device, that fails to work properly or fails to explode. 2. Adjective: Something that is ineffective,

worthless, or unsuccessful.   1. Noun: Failure, misfire, duffer, nonstarter. 2. Adjective: Ineffective, useless, worthless, unsuccessful.   1. The bomb disposal unit safely removed the dud grenade from the area. 2. Unfortunately, their plan turned out to be a dud, and they had to start over from scratch.   صاروخ فاشِل-فاشِل-
ذخيرة فاشلة أو عديمة المفعول

dupe   1. Noun: A person who is easily deceived or tricked; a fool. 2. Verb: To deceive or trick someone into believing something that is false.   1. Noun: Fool, sucker, gull, victim. 2. Verb: Deceive, trick, fool, mislead, hoodwink.   1. He realized too late that he had been a dupe in their scheme to sell fake artwork. 2. The con artist managed to dupe several investors into giving him large sums of money.   ضَحِيّة-ةخَدَعَ

duplicitous   describes someone who is deceitful or two-faced, often presenting one appearance or behavior while hiding a different, usually negative, intention or motive. Deceitful, dishonest, deceptive, hypocritical, insincere   His duplicitous behavior, pretending to support the project while secretly working against it, eventually led to distrust among the team members.
مُزَدَدِّري-ذي الوجهين

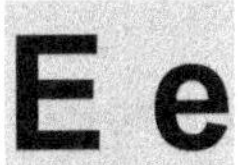

E e

ebullition   a sudden outburst or display of emotion, especially one that is intense or overwhelming. It can also refer to a sudden boiling or bubbling up of a liquid.
    Outburst, eruption, explosion, surge, boiling 1. The political debate quickly escalated into a heated ebullition of anger and accusations. 2. The ebullition of the water in the kettle signaled that it was ready for tea.
اِنْدِفَاع-ثَوَرَان-جَيَشَان

eccentric   1. Adjective: Unconventional, peculiar, or odd in behavior or appearance; deviating from the customary or expected norms. 2. Noun: A person who has unconventional or strange behavior; an odd or unconventional person.   1. Adjective: Quirky, peculiar, unconventional, odd, strange. 2. Noun: Oddball, nonconformist, maverick, individualist.   1. His eccentric taste in clothing always made him stand out at social gatherings. 2. The old man was known around town as an eccentric who spent his days collecting unusual items. غَرِيب الأَطْوَار-عَجِيب

eccentricity   the quality of being unconventional or peculiar in behavior or appearance, or the state of deviating from what is customary or expected.
    Quirkiness, peculiarity, oddity, strangeness, unconventionality   Her eccentricity was evident in the way she decorated her house with unusual art pieces and colors.   غَرَابَة

ecclesiastical   relates to anything pertaining to the Christian Church, its organization, or its clergy.

Churchly, religious, clerical, sacred
Ecclesiastical matters often involve discussions about church doctrine and governance.   كَنَسِي

edict   an official order or proclamation issued by a person in authority, especially a government or ruler.
Decree, proclamation, order, command, directive   The king issued an edict forbidding any public gatherings without prior permission.   مَرْسُوم

edifice a large, imposing building or structure, especially one that is impressive in size or appearance.
Building, structure, construction, monument, architecture   The old cathedral stands as a magnificent edifice of medieval architecture. بِنَاءٌ ضَخْم

eerie   something that is strange and frightening, often suggesting supernatural elements or an atmosphere of unease.   Spooky, creepy, unsettling, haunting, uncanny   As they walked through the deserted town at night, they couldn't shake the eerie feeling that they were being watched.   مُرْعِب

efface   1. To erase or remove something completely, especially from a surface. 2. To make oneself inconspicuous or humble.   1. Erase, delete, obliterate, wipe out. 2. Withdraw, retreat, recede.   1. The graffiti on the wall was effaced by diligent cleaners. 2. She tried to efface herself during the meeting, preferring to listen rather than speak. مَحَّى-طَمَسَ

effeminate   describes a man or boy who shows traits or behaviors traditionally associated with women or girls, often in a way that is considered stereotypical or culturally feminine.   Feminine, unmanly, girlish, womanish, delicate   His effeminate mannerisms, such as his soft voice and graceful gestures, sometimes led others to make unfair assumptions about his personality.   مُؤَنَّث-خَنَّث

effigy   a sculpture or model of a person, often made to mock or criticize them, especially by being hanged or burnt in public as a form of protest or expression of anger. Dummy, model, figure, statue, likeness   The protestors made an effigy of the politician and burned it in the town square to express their outrage. تَمْثَال تَمْثِيلِي

effluent   1. Noun: Liquid waste or sewage discharged into a river or the sea. 2. Adjective: Flowing out or forth; emanating.   1. Noun: Sewage, waste, discharge, runoff. 2. Adjective: Flowing, emanating, outgoing.   1. The company was fined for releasing untreated effluent into the nearby river. 2. The effluent gases from the factory contributed to air pollution in the surrounding area.   مِيَّاهُ صَرْف-مُنْبَعِث

effrontery   behavior that is bold, rude, or disrespectful, especially when one shows a lack of shame or embarrassment about one's actions.   Impudence, audacity, cheek, nerve, brazenness   His effrontery in asking for a raise after only a month on the job surprised everyone in the office.   وَقَاحَة

egg someone on   to urge or provoke someone to do something, especially something reckless, foolish, or daring, often by taunting or challenging them.

Encourage, provoke, incite, stimulate, challenge
The group of friends egged him on to try the
dangerous stunt despite knowing the risks involved.
حَرَّض َ شَخْص

egregious   describes something that is extremely
bad or shocking, usually in a noticeable and outstanding
way.   Flagrant, blatant, outrageous, shocking,
appalling   The company's egregious errors in
accounting led to a significant financial loss. فَظيع

Elegiac   1. Adjective: Relating to or characteristic of an
elegy, which is a mournful poem or piece of music,
typically written in remembrance of someone who has
died. 2. Noun: A poem or song that is elegiac in nature,
expressing sorrow or lamentation.   Mournful,
melancholic, sorrowful, lamenting, plaintive 1. The
elegiac tone of the novel captured the protagonist's
deep sense of loss and longing. 2. She composed an
elegiac poem in memory of her beloved grandmother.
رِثَاءِيّ-حزين

elicit   to draw out or evoke a response, information, or
reaction from someone, typically through questioning,
discussion, or other methods.Evoke, extract, obtain,
derive, bring out   The interviewer's skillful
questioning managed to elicit important details about
the candidate's previous work experience. اِسْتَخْرَج

elocution   the skill of clear and expressive speech,
especially in public speaking or formal presentation.
Articulation, pronunciation, rhetoric, delivery,
oration Her elocution was impeccable, captivating the

audience with her clear and persuasive speech.
التَأْدِيَةُ-إلِقاء

elope   to run away secretly in order to get married, especially without parental consent or approval.   Run away, escape, flee, abscond The young couple decided to elope to Las Vegas and get married without telling their families. يَهْرُبان لِلزَّوَاج

elopement   the act of running away secretly to get married, especially without parental consent or approval.   Runaway marriage, Clandestine marriage   Their elopement surprised everyone; they quietly married in a small chapel in the countryside.
الِهَرْبُ لِلزَّوَاج

elucidate   to make something clear, explain, or clarify by providing additional information or details.   Explain, clarify, expound, illuminate, interpret   She asked the professor to elucidate his theory further so that the students could better understand it.
شَرَّح

elusive   something that is difficult to find, achieve, understand, or remember, often because it is cleverly hidden or evasive.   Evasive, elusive, slippery, tricky, evanescent   The elusive suspect managed to evade capture for months despite an extensive manhunt by the police.   مُتَّرَاوِح-مُرَاوِغ

emaciation   the extreme thinness or wasting away of the body, typically due to disease, malnutrition, or starvation.   Wasting, thinness, gauntness, skeletal appearance   The emaciation of the prisoner after months of inadequate food and harsh conditions was alarming to the rescue team. النحافة المفرطة-ضُمُور

embargo an official ban on trade or other commercial activity with a particular country or group of countries. Ban, prohibition, restriction, blockade, sanction The government imposed an embargo on imports from the neighboring country due to political tensions. حَظْرٌ تِجَارِي

Ember a small, glowing piece of coal or wood in a dying fire. Coal, cinder, residue She stared into the embers of the campfire, lost in thought as the flames slowly died down. جَمْرَة

embrasure an opening or aperture in a thick wall or fortification, usually for shooting through, with sides sloping inward to widen the opening on the inside. Loophole, opening The soldiers positioned themselves behind the stone embrasure, ready to defend the castle from invaders. فَجْوَةٌ في الجدار

embryology the branch of biology and medicine that deals with the study of embryos and their development. Embryology explores the stages of development from fertilization to birth in various organisms. عِلْمُ الجَنِينِيَّة

eminently means to a high degree; prominently, notably, or conspicuously. Prominently, notably, conspicuously, outstandingly, remarkably She was eminently qualified for the position, with years of experience and exceptional skills in her field. بِشَكْلٍ بَارِز

empiricism   the theory that knowledge comes primarily from sensory experience and observation rather than from theory or intuition.   Observation, experimentalism, practicality, pragmatism   Empiricism emphasizes the importance of direct observation and experimentation in the scientific method.   التَجْرِيبِيَّة

empyrean   the highest heaven, believed in ancient cosmology to be the realm of pure fire or light, where the gods and blessed souls dwelt.   Celestial, heavenly, divine, ethereal   The poet described the beauty of the stars as if they were scattered across the empyrean sky. السماء العليا-باسق-عرش الله

enactment   the process of passing a law by a legislative body or the act of putting a law or regulation into effect.   Legislation, lawmaking, passage, adoption, implementation   The enactment of new environmental regulations was celebrated as a step towards protecting natural habitats.   تَشْرِيع

enamoured   (also spelled "enamored") means to be filled with love or affection for someone or something.   Fond, infatuated, captivated, smitten, charmed   He was deeply enamoured with her kindness and intelligence.   مَغْرَم

encase   means   to enclose or cover something completely, typically with a protective covering or container.   Cover, surround, envelop, enclose, box in   The fragile artifact was carefully encased in bubble wrap to protect it during shipping.   يُغْلَف

encephalization   the evolutionary process where the brain, particularly the cerebral cortex, becomes larger and more complex relative to body size, leading to increased cognitive abilities in animals, especially humans.   Encephalization is believed to have played a crucial role in the development of higher cognitive functions and intelligence in mammals.   تَوَسُّعُ الدِّماغِ

enchantment   the state of being under a spell or charm, often associated with magic or supernatural influence. It can also describe intense delight or fascination.   Charm, spell, magic, fascination, allure   The old book was said to contain spells of enchantment that could bring luck to those who possessed it.   سِحْر

encroach   to gradually intrude upon or take possession of someone else's rights, territory, or domain, especially in a way that is unwelcome or harmful.   Intrude, invade, trespass, infringe, impinge   The construction project began to encroach on the protected wildlife sanctuary, sparking protests from environmentalists.   يُعْتَدُ عَلَى-يتجَاوز- اِجْتَاح

encroachment   the act or process of gradually intruding upon or taking possession of someone else's rights, territory, or domain, especially in a way that is unwelcome or harmful.   Intrusion, invasion, trespassing, infringement, infringement   The encroachment of urban development into the natural habitats of wildlife has led to significant environmental concerns.   اِعْتِدَاء-تَجَاوُز-اِنتِهاك

encumber   to burden or weigh down someone or something with difficulties, responsibilities, or obligations.   Burden, hinder, impede, obstruct, weigh down   The excessive paperwork encumbered the progress of the project, delaying its completion.   أَثْقَل

endemic   1. Adjective: Native to a specific region or environment and not found naturally anywhere else. 2. Noun: A plant, animal, or disease that is native to and restricted to a particular geographical area. Native, indigenous, local, restricted, confined   1. The koala is endemic to Australia, meaning it is found naturally only in that country. 2. Malaria is endemic in certain regions where mosquitoes carrying the parasite are prevalent year-round.   مَحَلّي-مَنْتَشِرٌ بَيْنَ السُكَّان- متوطِّن

endow   1. (Finance): To provide a permanent source of income or property, typically through a donation or gift, especially to an institution like a university or charity. 2. To provide someone with a quality or ability.   1. Finance: Fund, grant, donate, contribute. 2. Provide, equip, bless, furnish.   1. The wealthy philanthropist decided to endow a scholarship fund at the university to support underprivileged students. 2. She was endowed with a sharp intellect and a gift for diplomacy, making her an effective negotiator.   هَبَةَ-رَزَق-أَعْطَى

enfeebled   describes something or someone that has been weakened physically, mentally, or morally.   Weakened, debilitated, frail, feeble, exhausted

After weeks of illness, he emerged from the hospital enfeebled but determined to regain his strength.   مُتَضَعَّف

engender   to cause or give rise to a feeling, situation, or condition, especially one that continues to exist or develop.   Generate, cause, produce, create, provoke   The divisive rhetoric of the politician served only to engender more distrust among the citizens.   أَثَّرَ

engirdle   To form a circle around; to encompass or surround something completely.   Surround, enclose, encompass, gird, circle   the cloud-engirdled peaks of the Andes   يُحَاطُ بِ-يطوّق

ennobles   to elevate someone to a higher rank or status, especially through noble or virtuous qualities.   Elevate, dignify, honor, uplift, ennoble   Her selfless dedication to charitable work ennobles her in the eyes of the community.   يُشَرِّف

ensconced   to settle comfortably or securely in a place, especially to establish oneself firmly or comfortably in a position or place.   Settle, install, lodge, establish, position   After years of hard work, she finally ensconced herself as the CEO of the company.   اِستَقَرّ-يستكن

enshrine   to preserve or protect something as if in a shrine, especially something considered sacred or valuable. It can also mean to cherish or honor something deeply.   Preserve, protect, treasure, honor, sanctify The constitution enshrines the

fundamental rights and freedoms of its citizens.
يُحْرِزُ-قدّس

entrancing   describes something that captures and holds the attention or imagination in a captivating or mesmerizing way.   Enchanting, captivating, mesmerizing, spellbinding, fascinating   The dancer's graceful movements were entrancing, leaving the audience spellbound.   سَاحِر-أَخَّاذ-فاتِن

environed   means surrounded or encircled by something.   Surrounded, encircled, encompassed, enclosed   The ancient castle was environed by a dense forest, making it difficult for intruders to approach unnoticed.   مُحَاط

envoy   a representative or messenger sent on a mission, especially one representing a government or a diplomatic mission.   Representative, messenger, delegate, emissary   The envoy was sent to negotiate a peace treaty between the two warring nations.   مَبْعُوث

epergne   an ornamental centerpiece for a dining table, typically used for holding fruit, flowers, or sweetmeats.   Centerpiece, ornament, table decoration, flower holder   The elegant epergne in the center of the dining table was filled with fresh flowers, adding a touch of beauty to the banquet.   حامِل زُخْرُفِي

ephemeral   lasting for a very short time.   Transient, fleeting, short-lived, momentary   The beauty of the sunrise was ephemeral, vanishing quickly as the sun rose higher in the sky.زائِل

epigram   a pithy, often witty, remark or short poem expressing an idea in a clever and amusing way.

Quip, aphorism, witticism, maxim   Oscar Wilde was known for his clever epigrams, which often contained sharp observations about society .

حِكْمَة مُوجَزَة

epistle   a formal or elegant letter, often used in the context of the letters found in the New Testament of the Bible. Letter, missive, communication, correspondence   The apostle Paul's epistle to the Corinthians is one of the most well-known letters in the New Testament.   رِسَالَة

epithet   a descriptive term or phrase expressing a quality or characteristic of the person or thing mentioned, often used as a term of abuse or contempt.

Nickname, label, designation, sobriquet
Alexander the Great is an epithet that reflects his extraordinary achievements and conquests.   لَقَب

equanimity   mental calmness, composure, and evenness of temper, especially in a difficult situation.

Composure, calmness, tranquility, poise
Despite the chaos around him, the doctor maintained his equanimity and performed the surgery with steady hands.   رَوَاذَة

equipage   the equipment or furnishings associated with a particular activity, especially a carriage and the horses, attendants, and other accessories associated with it. Equipment, apparatus, gear, accoutrements The royal equipage, complete with gilded carriages and well-dressed attendants, drew the admiration of the onlookers.   تَجْهِيزَات-عُدَّة

equivocal   means open to more than one interpretation, often intentionally so; ambiguous or uncertain.   Ambiguous, unclear, vague, dubious The politician's equivocal statement left the audience unsure of his true position on the issue.   مُبْهَم

equivocate   to use ambiguous language so as to conceal the truth or avoid committing oneself.
Prevaricate, hedge, be evasive, dodge
When asked directly about the scandal, the official began to equivocate, providing answers that were intentionally vague.   يُرَاوِغ-أَلْغَز-رَحرَح

erode   to gradually wear away or be worn away by natural forces such as wind, water, or ice.   Wear away, corrode, abrade, deteriorate   Over time, the relentless waves began to erode the cliffs, causing large chunks to fall into the sea.   يُتَآكَل

erosion   the process by which natural forces like water, wind, or ice gradually wear down and carry away soil, rock, or other material.   Wearing away, deterioration, abrasion, corrosion   The erosion of the riverbanks was accelerated by the heavy rains, leading to significant loss of farmland.   تَآكُل

errant   straying from the proper course or standards; erring or staying outside the proper path.   Wandering, straying, wayward, roving   The errant knight wandered through the countryside, seeking adventures and righting wrongs.   ضَالّ-شَارِد-تَائِه

erred   is the past tense of "err," which means to make a mistake or be incorrect.   Mistaken, blundered, miscalculated, misjudged He realized he had erred in his calculations, which caused the entire project to be delayed. أَخْطَأَ

erudite   having or showing great knowledge or learning.   Learned, scholarly, knowledgeable, well-read   The professor's erudite lecture on ancient philosophy captivated the students and left them eager to learn more. مُتَعَلِّم

erudition   the quality of having or showing great knowledge or learning; scholarship. Scholarship, learning, knowledge, intellect Her erudition was evident in her detailed analysis of the historical texts, which impressed even the most seasoned scholars.
ثَقَافَة-إطّلاع-إلمام

escapade   an adventurous, exciting, or somewhat daring act or experience.   Adventure, exploit, prank, misadventure Their weekend escapade to the mountains included rock climbing, rafting, and camping under the stars.   مُغَامَرَة

esoteric   intended for or likely to be understood by only a small number of people with a specialized knowledge or interest.Obscure, arcane, cryptic, abstruse, occult   The professor's lecture on quantum mechanics was so esoteric that only a few students could grasp the complex concepts. بَاطِنِيّ-سِرّيّ

espionage   the practice of spying or using spies to obtain information about the plans and activities, especially of a foreign government or competing company.   Spying, intelligence gathering, undercover work, surveillance   The novel's plot revolved around a high-stakes game of espionage, where double agents and secret missions kept readers on the edge of their seats.   تَجَسُّس

ethos   the characteristic spirit, moral values, beliefs, and attitudes of a community, culture, or era, often influencing the practices and behaviors of its members.   Spirit, character, culture, values   The company's ethos of innovation and customer satisfaction has helped it become a leader in the technology industry.   أَخْلاَقِيَّات-روح الجماعة-سمات تراثية مميزة

eudemonism   a philosophical theory that defines moral action as that which leads to the well-being, happiness, or flourishing of the individual.   Ethical happiness, well-being, moral happiness, flourishing The philosopher argued that eudemonism provides a more comprehensive understanding of ethics by emphasizing the pursuit of personal well-being and happiness.   السَّعَادَة الأَخْلاَقِيَّة

evade   to escape or avoid, especially by cleverness or trickery.   Elude, avoid, dodge, escape   The thief managed to evade the police by blending into the crowded marketplace. يَتَجَنَّب

evasively   in a manner intended to avoid giving a direct answer or to avoid committing oneself.   Elusively, ambiguously, indirectly, equivocally

When asked about his involvement in the project, he responded evasively, leaving everyone unsure of his true role. بِمُرَاوَغَة

evocate to call forth or evoke, often used to describe the act of bringing to mind strong memories, feelings, or images. Evoke, summon, conjure, invoke The artist's paintings are evocative, as they powerfully evoke the beauty and nostalgia of rural life. يَسْتَحْضِر-يثير

evocative bringing strong images, memories, or feelings to mind. Suggestive, reminiscent, expressive, haunting The old photographs were evocative of her childhood, filling her with a sense of nostalgia and warmth. مُثير لِلذِّكْرَيَات

exalt to raise in rank, honor, power, character, or quality; to praise highly or glorify. Glorify, elevate, praise, uplift The community gathered to exalt the local hero who had saved several lives during the natural disaster. يُجَلِّي

excision the act of removing or cutting out something, typically used in a medical context to describe the surgical removal of tissue. Removal, extraction, deletion, cutting out The surgeon performed an excision of the tumor to prevent it from spreading further. اِسْتِئْصَال

excrescence an abnormal outgrowth or enlargement, often used to describe an unwanted or disfiguring addition. Outgrowth, growth, protuberance, lump   The tree was covered in strange excrescences that made its bark look knotted and deformed.   نَتُوء

exert   to apply or bring to bear (a force, influence, or quality).   Apply, utilize, wield, exercise She had to exert a lot of effort to move the heavy furniture across the room.   يُبْذَل

exhortation   an address or communication emphatically urging someone to do something.   Urging, encouragement, admonition, persuasion The coach's passionate exhortation inspired the team to give their best performance in the final match.   حَثّ-عِظَة

expatriate   a person who lives outside their native country, often for a long period.   Exile, emigrant, non-native, migrant   As an expatriate, she had to adjust to a new culture and language while living in France for her job.   مُغْتَرِب

expedient   means of attaining an end, especially one that is convenient but considered improper or immoral.   Convenient, advantageous, practical, opportune   Although it was expedient to cut corners on the project, they knew it would ultimately lead to subpar results.   مُلائِم

expenditure   the act of spending money or the amount of money spent.   Spending, outlay, expense, disbursement The company's expenditure on research and development has significantly increased over the past year to foster innovation.   إِنْفَاق

expostulation an expression of earnest opposition or protest. Protest, objection, remonstration, disapproval Despite his vehement expostulation, the council decided to proceed with the controversial policy change. اِحْتِجَاج

expropriation the act of taking away property from its owner, typically for public use or benefit, often without the owner's consent. Confiscation, seizure, appropriation, requisition The government's expropriation of the farmland caused widespread discontent among the local farmers. مُصَادَرَة

extradite to hand over (a person accused or convicted of a crime) to the jurisdiction of the foreign state in which the crime was committed. Deport, hand over, transfer, repatriate The fugitive was arrested in a neighboring country, and the authorities agreed to extradite him to face charges in his home country. يُسَلّم لِدَوْلَة أُخْرَى

extraneous irrelevant or unrelated to the subject being dealt with; coming from outside or not essential. Irrelevant, unrelated, unconnected, external The editor removed all extraneous information from the article to ensure that the main points were clear and concise. غَيْر ذِي صِلَة

extrapolation the act of estimating or concluding something by assuming that existing trends will continue or a current method will remain applicable. Inference, projection, estimation, prediction The scientist made an extrapolation based on the current data, predicting future climate changes with remarkable accuracy. اِسْتِرْنَادَاج

extricate   to free (someone or something) from a constraint or difficulty. Free, release, disentangle, liberate   The firefighters worked tirelessly to extricate the survivors from the wreckage of the collapsed building. يُخَلِّصٌ-خَلَّصٌ-اِنْدَشَلَ

exuded   to discharge (moisture or a smell) slowly and steadily; to display (an emotion or quality) strongly and openly.   Emitted, discharged, radiated, oozed   She exuded confidence as she stepped onto the stage, captivating the audience with her presence. أَفَاضَ

F f

facetiousness a quality of treating serious issues with deliberately inappropriate humor; flippancy.   Flippancy, levity, joking, jesting   His facetiousness during the meeting was not appreciated, as the topic was of a very serious nature.   مُزَاح

fad an intense and widely shared enthusiasm for something, especially one that is short-lived and without basis in the object's qualities; a craze. Craze, trend, fashion, whim   The new diet quickly became a fad, with everyone rushing to try it despite its dubious health claims.   هَوَس مُؤَقَّت-بَدعَة

falsetto a method of voice production used by male singers, especially tenors, to sing notes higher than their normal range.   High-pitched voice, head voice, tenor   The singer impressed the audience with his ability to switch seamlessly into a clear falsetto during the performance.   صَوْت مُرتَفِع مُصطَنَع-صوت شديد الحدة

farce a comic dramatic work using buffoonery and horseplay, typically including crude characterization and ludicrously improbable situations.   Comedy, slapstick, mockery, absurdity   The play was a hilarious farce, filled with exaggerated characters and ridiculous situations that kept the audience laughing throughout.   مَلْهَاة-مَهزَلَة

farcical relating to or resembling a farce, especially because of absurd or ridiculous aspects.

Absurd, ridiculous, ludicrous, preposterous The entire situation became farcical when the supposedly serious debate turned into a shouting match filled with outlandish accusations.   مَهْزَلِي

farrago   a confused mixture or hodgepodge of things.   Mixture, jumble, hodgepodge, medley   The lecture was a farrago of unrelated topics, leaving the students confused and overwhelmed.
مَزِيج

farthingale   a hooped petticoat or framework used in the 16th and 17th centuries to extend the skirt.
          Hooped petticoat, crinoline, underskirt, hoop skirt   The noblewoman's elaborate gown was supported by a farthingale, giving it a wide and graceful silhouette.   التَّنّورَةُ المُقَوَّسَة

fastidiousness   the quality of being very attentive to and concerned about accuracy and detail; meticulousness.   Meticulousness, precision, exactitude, thoroughness   Her fastidiousness in organizing the event ensured that everything went off without a hitch.   دِقَّة

fealty   a feudal tenant's or vassal's sworn loyalty to a lord; fidelity or allegiance.   Loyalty, allegiance, fidelity, devotion   The knight pledged his fealty to the king, vowing to serve and protect him faithfully.
وَلاء-طاعَة

fecundity   the ability to produce an abundance of offspring or new growth; fertility.   Fertility, fruitfulness, productivity, prolificacy   The fecundity of the farmland was evident in the bountiful harvest that it produced each year. خِصْب

feign   to pretend to be affected by (a feeling, state, or injury). Pretend, simulate, fake, fabricate   She tried to feign indifference when she heard the news, but her true emotions were evident. يَتَظَاهَر

felicitous   1. well-chosen or suited to the circumstances. 2. pleasing and fortunate.   1. Appropriate, suitable, apt, fitting. 2. fortunate, pleasing, happy. 1. His felicitous choice of words made his speech memorable and impactful. 2. the view was the room's only felicitous feature. مُلائِم-لَبِق-رائِع

Felicity   1. the ability to find appropriate expression for one's thoughts. 2. intense happiness.   1. eloquence, aptness, appropriateness, appropriacy, suitability. 2. Happiness, bliss, joy, delight   1. he exposed the kernel of the matter with his customary elegance and felicity. 2. Their wedding day was filled with felicity, as family and friends gathered to celebrate their union.   سَعَادَة-لَبَاقَة

festering   a wound or sore becoming septic; suppurating. It can also mean a negative feeling or a problem becoming worse or more intense, especially through long-term neglect or indifference. Suppurating, ulcerating, rotting, decaying   The festering wound required immediate medical attention to prevent further infection.   تَقَرُّح

fettered   restrained with chains or manacles, typically around the ankles; to be restricted or confined.

Shackled, chained, bound, restrained   The prisoner was fettered to the wall, unable to move more than a few feet in any direction. مُقَيَّد

fiasco   a complete and ignominious failure, especially in a ludicrous or humiliating way.   Disaster, debacle, failure, catastrophe   The poorly planned event turned into a fiasco, with guests leaving early and the organizers scrambling to fix multiple issues. فَشَل ذَرِيع

flagitious   criminal, villainous, or wicked; extremely brutal or heinous.   Heinous, atrocious, nefarious, vile   The dictator's flagitious acts against his own people shocked the international community.   شِنِيع

flagrant   conspicuously or obviously offensive; blatant.   Blatant, glaring, obvious, egregious The referee ignored the flagrant foul, which caused an uproar among the fans.   فَاضِح

flay   peel the skin off (a corpse or carcass) or to criticize someone severely and brutally.   Skin, strip, excoriate, lash The harsh critic would often flay new authors in his reviews, leaving their reputations in tatters. يَسْلُخ

fledgling   a young bird that has just fledged or learned to fly; it can also mean a person or organization that is immature, inexperienced, or underdeveloped.   Newcomer, novice, beginner, rookie The fledgling company faced many challenges in its first year, but it eventually found its footing in the competitive market.   فَرْخ-غِرّ-ساذج-ناشئة

flunkey   a person who performs menial tasks for someone else, often in an obsequious manner. The term can also refer to someone who is excessively subservient or eager to please.   Servant, lackey, minion, underling, toady   Despite his impressive title, many saw him as nothing more than a flunkey to the powerful CEO, always ready to do her bidding without question.   خَادِم

fluorescence   the emission of light by a substance that has absorbed light or other electromagnetic radiation. It is a form of luminescence, typically seen when a substance emits visible light after being exposed to ultraviolet light.   Luminescence, glow, radiance, phosphorescence, emission   The scientist observed the fluorescence of the mineral sample under ultraviolet light, noting its brilliant green glow. تَأَلُّق ضَوْئِي

foist   to impose something unwelcome or unnecessary on someone, often by deceit or without their knowledge or consent.   Impose, force, thrust, offload, palm off   The salesman tried to foist a substandard product on the unsuspecting customer, claiming it was the latest model.   يَفْرِض

footman   a male servant, especially one who serves at table, opens the door, and runs errands. Historically, a footman was often part of the household staff in a large estate. Servant, attendant, butler, manservant, steward The footman promptly opened the grand doors of the mansion as the guests arrived for the evening gala. خَدَّام-خادِم

forasmuch   an archaic term used to mean "since" or "because," often found in older legal or formal texts.   Since, because, considering that, inasmuch as, seeing that   Forasmuch as he had already completed his studies, he decided to take a well-deserved vacation.   بِمَا أَن

forbearance   the act of refraining from exercising a legal right, especially enforcing the payment of a debt. It can also mean patience, self-control, and restraint in difficult situations.   Patience, restraint, tolerance, endurance, self-control   The lender showed great forbearance by giving the borrower additional time to repay the loan without imposing any penalties.
تَحَلٍّ بِالصَّبْر-رَحَابَةُ الصَّدْر-تَسَامُح

forbore   is the past tense of "forbear," which means to refrain from doing something, especially by exercising self-control.   Refrained, abstained, withheld, avoided, resisted   Despite his anger, he forbore from making any harsh comments during the meeting.
اِمْتَنَع-أَحْجَم

forego   to go before or precede. It is often confused with "forgo," which means to do without or abstain from.   Precede, antecede, lead up to, come before, pave the way for   The introduction will forego the main presentation, providing essential context and background.   يَسْبِق

foreshadowing   a literary device in which a writer gives an advance hint of what is to come later in the story. It often helps to build anticipation and tension.   Hinting, predicting, presaging, suggesting,

foretelling   The dark clouds gathering on the horizon were a foreshadowing of the impending storm that would change their lives forever.   ُالتَّدْبِيهُ المُسْبَق

forgo to do without something, to abstain or refrain from something that one might want or need. Renounce, relinquish, waive, abstain, eschew   She decided to forgo dessert to maintain her diet.   يْتَخَلَّى عَن

forsworn   is the past participle of "forswear," which means 1. to renounce or reject something strongly, especially with an oath. 2. or to be guilty of perjury; swear falsely. Renounced, rejected, abjured, disavowed, repudiated   1. the country has not forsworn nuclear weapons. 2. I swore that I would lead us safely home and I do not mean to be forsworn.   نبذت-
تعهّد بنبذه-يُقسِم كاذبًا-خنث بقسمة

fortitude   mental and emotional strength in facing adversity, danger, or temptation with courage and resilience.   Courage, bravery, resilience, endurance, steadfastness Her fortitude in the face of illness inspired everyone around her.   ثَبَات-تَحَمّل-صَبَر

fratricidal   the act of killing one's own brother or sister, or relating to such an act. It can also metaphorically describe conflict within a group or nation.   Brother-killing, internecine, destructive, fraternal conflict, familial slaughter   The civil war descended into a fratricidal conflict, pitting neighbor against neighbor in a bitter struggle. قَاتِلُ الإِخْوَةِ-صراع الأخوة

fray   1. a noisy fight, battle, or skirmish. 2. the act of becoming worn at the edge, typically through constant rubbing.   1. Fight, conflict, brawl, scuffle, skirmish. 2. become worn, ragged, shabby.   1. As tensions rose, the heated debate quickly turned into a fray, with participants shouting over one another. 2. cheap fabric soon frays.   مُشاجَرة-أَبْلَى

frigidly   in a very cold manner, either literally or figuratively. It can describe both physical coldness and a cold, unfriendly demeanor. Coldly, icily, unfriendly, frostily, unwelcomingly   She spoke frigidly to her former friend, making it clear that their relationship was beyond repair. بِبُرُودَة

fringes   the outer edges or borders of an area, group, or activity. It can also refer to decorative edging on fabric or clothing. Edges, borders, peripheries, outskirts, margins   The community theater troupe operated on the fringes of the city's cultural scene, attracting a dedicated but small audience.   أَطْرَاف

frivolity   behavior that is silly, light-hearted, or lacking in seriousness. It often implies a lack of necessary seriousness or maturity. Levity, silliness, lightheartedness, playfulness, triviality   The party was filled with laughter and frivolity, providing a much-needed break from the stresses of everyday life.   خِفَّة-رُعُونَة

frivolousness   the quality of being carefree and not serious, often in a way that is considered inappropriate or unnecessary given the circumstances.   Levity,

silliness, triviality, lightheartedness, flippancy
His frivolousness during the important meeting was frowned upon by his colleagues, who expected a more professional attitude. خِفَّة-تَّهوّر

fructify   to make fruitful or productive, or to bear fruit.   Fertilize, yield, produce, bear fruit, enrich   The innovative farming techniques helped the arid land to fructify, turning it into a lush and productive field.   يُثْمِر

frugal   being economical or thrifty, especially in terms of spending money or using resources. It implies a careful and efficient use of resources.   Thrifty, economical, sparing, prudent, cost-conscious   Living a frugal lifestyle allowed her to save enough money for her dream vacation without going into debt.   مُقْتَصِد

frugality   the quality of being economical with resources, particularly with money, and avoiding waste. Thriftiness, economy, prudence, parsimony, sparingness, tightfistedness   His frugality enabled him to retire early, having saved diligently throughout his career.   تَقَشُّف

fruition   the realization or accomplishment of a plan or project. It can also mean the point at which something comes to a successful conclusion or reaches its desired outcome.   Realization, fulfillment, achievement, completion, consummation   After years of hard work and dedication, the project finally came to fruition, exceeding everyone's expectations.   تَحْقِيق

fulcrum   the support or point on which a lever pivots. In a broader sense, it can also refer to the central or most important part of a situation, activity, or event. Pivot, hinge, support, cornerstone, central point   The new policy became the fulcrum around which the company's restructuring efforts were balanced.   نُقْطَةُ الارْتِكَاز

furnace   an enclosed structure in which material can be heated to very high temperatures, typically for the purpose of heating a building or for industrial processes such as smelting or refining.   Heater, boiler, kiln, stove, incinerator   The old furnace finally broke down in the middle of winter, leaving the family to endure the cold until a repairman could arrive.   فُرْن

furore   an outbreak of public anger or excitement. It can also mean a state of intense activity or agitation.   Uproar, commotion, frenzy, outcry, turmoil   The controversial decision by the government caused a furore among the citizens, leading to protests in the streets.   ضَجَّة

furtive   attempting to avoid notice or attention, typically because of guilt or a belief that discovery would lead to trouble. It implies stealthiness and secrecy.   Secretive, stealthy, sneaky, clandestine, surreptitious   She cast a furtive glance over her shoulder, hoping no one would notice her slipping the letter into her bag.   خَفِي

G g

gait   a person's manner of walking or moving on foot. It can also apply to the movement patterns of animals.   Walk, stride, pace, step, locomotion   Her graceful gait was the result of years of ballet training, evident in every step she took.   مِشْيَة

gaiter   a garment worn over the shoe and lower pants leg, typically used for protection against mud, water, or debris. It can also refer to a covering for the ankle and lower leg.   Legging, spats, puttee, protective covering, overshoe   Hikers often wear gaiters to keep their boots and pants dry and clean while trekking through wet or muddy terrain.غِطَاء السَّاق

galvanize   to shock or excite someone into taking action. It can also refer to coating iron or steel with a protective layer of zinc to prevent rusting.   Stimulate, spur, provoke, incite, rouse   The urgent call for volunteers galvanized the community into action, resulting in a record number of people signing up to help.   يُحَفِّز

gangrene   the death of body tissue due to a lack of blood flow or a severe bacterial infection. It typically affects extremities like fingers, toes, and limbs but can also occur in muscles and organs.   Tissue death, necrosis, decay, mortification, putrefaction   The severe frostbite led to gangrene in his toes, necessitating immediate medical intervention to prevent the spread of infection.   غَرْغَرِينَا

garland   a decorative wreath or cord, often made of flowers, leaves, or other materials, typically used as an ornament or symbol of honor.   Wreath, festoon, lei, chaplet, coronet   The bride wore a beautiful garland of fresh flowers on her head, adding a touch of natural elegance to her wedding attire.   إِكْلِيل

garnered   to gather or collect something, especially information or approval.   Collected, gathered, accumulated, amassed, acquired   The scientist garnered significant data from the experiment, which contributed to a breakthrough in her research.   جَمَع

gasjet   a nozzle or opening from which gas is released, commonly used in gas stoves, heaters, or lamps to produce a controlled flame. Burner, nozzle, gas burner, gas outlet, jet   She adjusted the gas jet on the stove to ensure the flame was at the right intensity for simmering the sauce.   فُوَّهة الغاز

gelatinous   a substance that has a jelly-like consistency.   Jelly-like, gooey, viscous, slimy, glutinous   The scientist noted the gelatinous texture of the new compound, which resembled a thick, translucent gel.   هُلامِي

gentry   people of good social position, specifically the class of people next below the nobility in position and birth in England.   Upper class, aristocracy, nobility, elite, upper crust   The old manor was home to the local gentry, who often hosted lavish parties for the neighboring estates.   طَبَقَةُ النُّبَلَاء

gerrymander   the practice of manipulating the boundaries of an electoral constituency to favor one party or class. Manipulate, rig, distort, falsify, skew The political party was accused of trying to gerrymander the district boundaries to ensure their continued dominance in the elections. اَلتَّلَاعُبُ بِالحُدُودِ الِانْتِخَابِيَّة

gewgaws   showy but worthless or useless trinkets or ornaments. Baubles, trinkets, knickknacks, doodads, gimcracks   The souvenir shop was filled with gewgaws that attracted tourists but held little real value. أَلْعَاب تَافِهَة

gibbous   the phase of the moon when it is more than half but less than fully illuminated, appearing swollen or rounded.   Swollen, bulging, convex, rounded, humpbacked   The gibbous moon cast a soft glow over the landscape, creating an ethereal and mysterious atmosphere.   أَحْدَب

gilded   covered thinly with gold leaf or gold paint. It can also refer to something that appears valuable or attractive on the surface but may be lacking in true value or quality.   Gold-plated, golden, ornate, embellished, luxurious   The grand ballroom was adorned with gilded mirrors and chandeliers, exuding an air of opulence and grandeur. مُذَهَّب

glide   to move smoothly, effortlessly, and often gracefully.   Slide, float, sail, skim, drift   The ice skater seemed to glide across the rink, her movements fluid and elegant.   يَنْزَلِق

gloats   to dwell on one's own success or another's misfortune with smugness or malignant pleasure.
Boasts, brags, revels, exults, delights   He couldn't help but gloat over his victory in the chess match, much to the annoyance of his opponent.
يَشْمَت

glut   an excessive supply of something, often leading to a surplus that exceeds demand.   Surplus, oversupply, excess, abundance, overflow   The sudden glut of smartphones on the market caused prices to drop significantly.   فائِض

glutted   having an excessive supply of something, often to the point of saturation.
Oversupplied, saturated, overfilled, flooded, inundated   The market was glutted with cheap imports, making it difficult for local businesses to compete.   مُشَبَّع

glutton   a person who eats and drinks excessively or voraciously. It can also refer to someone who has an insatiable appetite for something, such as work or a particular activity.   Overeater, gourmand, voracious eater, binge eater, hog
Despite being warned about the health risks, he remained a glutton, indulging in large quantities of rich, fatty foods.   نَهِم

gluttony   excessive eating and drinking, often to the point of wastefulness or overindulgence. It is considered one of the seven deadly sins in Christian theology.   Overindulgence, greed, voracity, excess, bingeing   His gluttony at the banquet was evident, as he piled his plate high with food and returned for multiple servings.   الشَّرَه

goaded   to provoke or annoy someone so as to stimulate some action or reaction. It can also mean to drive or urge an animal to move forward.   Provoked, incited, spurred, prodded, urged   He was goaded into action by his rival's taunts, determined to prove himself once and for all.   مُسْتَفَز

gorging   eating a large amount greedily; filling oneself with food.   Stuffing, devouring, feasting, overeating, binging   During the holiday feast, everyone was gorging on the delicious dishes, unable to resist the abundant spread.   نَهَم

gormandising   to eat greedily or ravenously, often with an emphasis on fine or rich food.   Gluttonizing, devouring, feasting, indulging, bingeing   He spent the evening gormandising at the buffet, savoring every gourmet dish on offer.   التَّهام

grafting   the horticultural technique of joining two plants together so they grow as one. In a broader sense, it can also mean incorporating or transplanting something into a different context.   Splicing, joining, fusing, uniting, combining   The gardener was skilled at grafting different varieties of apple trees to create a single tree that bore multiple types of apples.   تَطْعِيم

granary   a storehouse or room in a barn for threshed grain or animal feed.   Silo,

storehouse, repository, warehouse, grain bin   The
farmers stored their harvested wheat in the granary to
keep it safe from the elements and pests.   مَخْزَنُ
الحُبُوب

grapple   to engage in a close fight or struggle
without weapons; to wrestle. It can also mean to
struggle with a difficult problem or situation. Wrestle,
struggle, tussle, contend, wrest   The two
opponents grappled fiercely in the ring, each trying to
gain the upper hand. يُصارِع

gratis   given or done for free, without charge or
payment.   Free, complimentary, costless, unpaid,
without charge The restaurant offered water and bread
gratis to all its diners, regardless of what they ordered.
مَجَّانا

gratuitous   uncalled for, lacking good reason, or
unwarranted. It can also refer to something given or
done free of charge.   Unwarranted, unnecessary,
unjustified, unprovoked, needless   The film was
criticized for its gratuitous violence, which many felt was
included only for shock value. غَيْرُ مُبَرَّر

grille a grating or screen of metal bars or wires,
typically used to cover an opening for protection or
ventilation.   Grating, screen, mesh, lattice, grate
The old mansion's windows were covered with ornate
iron grilles, adding to its mysterious charm. شَبَاكك

gripes   complaints or grumbles about something,
especially minor or persistent complaints.
        Complaints, grievances, moans, grumbles,

objections   Despite the team's victory, the coach had a few gripes about their defensive strategy and lack of coordination. شَكَاوَى

groat   an old English coin, worth four pence, which was used from the 14th to the 17th centuries. It can also refer to hulled or crushed grain, especially oats.
    Coin, fourpence, penny, grain, oat   In medieval England, a groat could buy a substantial amount of goods at the local market.   غرُوشة

grotesque   something that is comically or repulsively ugly or distorted. It can also describe anything that is incongruous or inappropriate to a shocking degree.
    Hideous, monstrous, bizarre, distorted, outlandish   The artist's latest sculpture was a grotesque figure with exaggerated features that left many viewers feeling uneasy.   غَرِيب

grovel   act in an excessively submissive or humble manner, often out of fear or to gain favor. It can also refer to lying or crawling on the ground, especially in abject humility.   Cower, cringe, kneel, prostrate, abase oneself Desperate to keep his job, he began to grovel before his boss, apologizing profusely for his mistakes.   يَتَذَلَّل

gudgeon   a small European freshwater fish often used as bait. It can also refer to a gullible person who is easily deceived or cheated.   Baitfish, dupe, fool, sucker, pawn He was such a gudgeon that he fell for every scam email that landed in his inbox.   مُغَفَّل

guillotine   a machine with a heavy blade sliding vertically in grooves, used for beheading people. It can also refer to any method of cutting or dividing quickly and decisively.   Beheading machine, decapitator, chopper, cutter, execution device   During the French Revolution, many political prisoners met their end at the guillotine in the public squares of Paris.   مِقْصَلَة

guinea   a former British gold coin that was minted between 1663 and 1813, worth 21 shillings. The term is also used to refer to the equivalent amount in British currency, especially in auction and professional fees.   Gold coin, British currency, sovereign, pound, shilling   The antique vase was sold for five guineas at the auction, reflecting its high value and rarity.   جِنِيه ذَهَبِي

gullible   someone who is easily deceived or tricked because they are too trusting or naive.   Naive, credulous, trusting, unsuspecting, easily fooled   The con artist found it easy to swindle the gullible tourists with his elaborate scams.   ساذِج

gushed   to flow out rapidly and in large quantities. It can also describe speaking or expressing oneself in an overly enthusiastic or effusive manner.   Spurted, streamed, poured, erupted, effused   Tears gushed from her eyes as she read the heartfelt letter from her long-lost friend.   تَدَفَّق

gusts   are brief, strong bursts of wind.   Blasts, squalls, gales, flurries, bursts   The sudden gusts of

wind made it difficult to keep the umbrella steady during
the storm.   هَبَّات

gypsum   a soft sulfate mineral composed of
calcium sulfate dihydrate, used in a variety of
applications including drywall, plaster, and fertilizer.
Calcium sulfate, alabaster, selenite, mineral, plaster
rock   The sculptor used gypsum to create detailed
molds for his latest artwork.   جِبْس

H h

hackney   originally refers to a horse suitable for ordinary riding or driving. Over time, it has come to mean something that is overused to the point of losing its original meaning or significance, becoming trite or clichéd.   Cliché, trite, overused, commonplace, banal   The hackneyed phrases in his speech failed to inspire the audience, who had heard them all before. مُبْتَذَل

hamstrung   to severely restrict the efficiency or effectiveness of something or someone. The term originates from the practice of cutting the hamstring of a horse to render it lame.   Crippled, hindered, handicapped, incapacitated, obstructed   The company's growth was hamstrung by outdated technology and a lack of skilled workers.   مُقَيَّد

hankering   a strong desire or longing for something.   Yearning, craving, longing, desire, urge   After months of healthy eating, she had a hankering for a slice of rich, chocolate cake. تَوْق

haptic   relates to the sense of touch, particularly involving the perception and manipulation of objects using the hands.   Tactile, touch-based, kinesthetic, tangible, sensory   The new virtual reality system includes haptic feedback to simulate the sensation of touching objects in the virtual world. لَمْسِي

harangue   a lengthy and aggressive speech or lecture, often delivered with strong emotion. Tirade, rant, diatribe, lecture, admonition   The politician's harangue about government corruption lasted for nearly an hour, leaving the audience both impressed and exhausted.   خُطْبَة

harnessing   the act of controlling and making use of a resource or force for a particular purpose.   Utilizing, exploiting, employing, channeling, leveraging   The engineers focused on harnessing solar energy to provide a sustainable power source for the entire community.   تَسْخِير

harping   dwelling on or repeatedly discussing a particular subject in a tiresome or annoying way. Nagging, dwelling, reiterating, obsessing, fixating   He kept harping on the same old issues, much to the annoyance of his friends who had already moved on.
التَّكْرَار المُزْعِج

havoc   widespread destruction or chaos. Devastation, destruction, chaos, disorder, mayhem The hurricane wreaked havoc on the coastal town, leaving buildings destroyed and streets flooded.   دَمَار

hearken   to listen attentively or give heed to something.   Listen, attend, heed, pay attention, observe   The wise old man advised the villagers to hearken to the signs of nature to predict the weather.
يُذْصِت

hearsay   information received from other people that one cannot adequately substantiate; rumor. Gossip, rumor, unverified information, secondhand information, report.   The judge dismissed the witness's statement as hearsay since it was not based on their own knowledge.   شائِعات

hearth   the floor of a fireplace, often extending into a room and usually made of stone or brick. It can also refer to the area in front of a fireplace or the symbol of home and family life. Fireplace, fireside, home, abode, hearthstone.   They gathered around the hearth on cold winter nights to share stories and keep warm.   مَوقِد

hedonist   a person who believes that the pursuit of pleasure is the most important thing in life; a pleasure-seeker.   Pleasure-seeker, sybarite, sensualist, epicurean, bon vivant.As a hedonist, she spent her weekends indulging in gourmet food and luxurious spa treatments.   مُتَلَذِّذ

hedonistic   a way of life or attitude that is primarily focused on the pursuit of pleasure and self-indulgence.   Pleasure-seeking, self-indulgent, sybaritic, sensual, epicurean.   Their hedonistic lifestyle was marked by extravagant parties and lavish vacations.   مُتَلَذِّذي

held-sway-over   to have great control or influence over someone or something. Dominated, controlled, ruled, governed, influenced.   The charismatic leader held sway over the entire organization, guiding its direction and decisions.   سَيْطَرَ على

heresy   a belief or opinion that is contrary to the orthodox religious doctrine, especially that of a church or religious system. It can also refer to any belief or theory that is strongly at variance with established

beliefs, customs, or traditions.   Dissent, nonconformity, heterodoxy, apostasy, unorthodoxy. The scientist was accused of heresy for challenging the traditional views of the academic community.
بِدْعَة

heretic   a person who holds beliefs or opinions that are contrary to the established doctrines of a religion, particularly Christianity, or any other established system or institution.   Dissenter, nonconformist, apostate, schismatic, iconoclast. The church excommunicated the heretic for his radical views that opposed their teachings. مُبْتَدِع

heritable   traits, properties, or rights that can be passed from parents to their offspring through inheritance.   Inheritable, genetic, transmissible, inheritable, passed down.   The genetic disorder was heritable, affecting multiple generations in the family.
وَرَاثِي

hermit   a person who lives in seclusion from society, often for religious or spiritual reasons.   Recluse, solitary, ascetic, anchorite, loner.   The old hermit lived alone in a small cabin deep in the woods, far away from the hustle and bustle of city life. ناسِك

heterodoxy   beliefs, opinions, or doctrines that deviate from accepted or orthodox standards, particularly in religion.   Unorthodoxy, dissent, nonconformity, heresy, iconoclasm. His heterodoxy was evident in his unconventional interpretations of religious texts, which often sparked controversy among his peers.   غَيْر أَرْثُوذُكْسِيَّة

heterogeneous refers to something that is diverse in character or content, consisting of different or diverse elements. Diverse, varied, mixed, assorted, eclectic. The city's population is quite heterogeneous, with people from various ethnic backgrounds and cultures. مُتَنَوِّع

hiatus a pause or gap in a sequence, series, or process. Pause, break, interruption, gap, intermission. After a two-year hiatus, the band reunited to release a new album and go on tour. فَتْرَة انْقِطاع

hither and thither an expression meaning to move in various directions, often in a disorganized or aimless manner. Here and there, to and fro, in all directions, back and forth, everywhere. The children ran hither and thither in the park, enjoying their freedom on a sunny afternoon. هُنا وَهُناك

hodgepodge a confused mixture or jumble of different things. Mixture, jumble, medley, mishmash, assortment. Her bookshelf was a hodgepodge of novels, textbooks, magazines, and personal mementos. خَلِيط

holistic the idea that systems and their properties should be viewed as wholes, not just as a collection of parts. In medicine, it considers the whole person, including mental and social factors, rather than just physical symptoms. Comprehensive, integrative, inclusive, whole, complete. The doctor took a holistic approach to treatment, addressing not only the physical symptoms but also the patient's emotional and mental well-being. شُمُولِي

hoodwink   to deceive or trick someone.   Deceive, trick, dupe, mislead, fool.   The scammer tried to hoodwink people into giving their personal information by pretending to be a bank representative. يَخْدَع

hovel   a small, squalid, and often poorly constructed dwelling.   Shack, shanty, hut, cabin, slum. The family lived in a tiny hovel on the outskirts of the city, with barely enough room for their basic needs. كَوْخ

hubbub   a chaotic noise caused by a crowd of people; a busy and noisy situation.   Uproar, commotion, clamor, din, racket.   The marketplace was filled with the hubbub of vendors shouting and customers bargaining.   ضَجَّة

hue   a color or shade.   Color, shade, tint, tone, pigment.   The artist carefully selected hues of blue and green to create a tranquil seascape.   لَوْن

hullabaloo   a loud noise or uproar, especially one caused by a lot of people excitedly talking or shouting.   Commotion, uproar, clamor, fuss, ruckus.   There was a great hullabaloo in the streets after the team won the championship.   جَلَبَة

humbugs   deceptive or false talk or behavior, often used to trick or deceive people. It can also refer to people who engage in such behavior.   Deceit, trickery, deception, fraud, impostors. The politician's promises turned out to be nothing more than humbugs, leaving the voters feeling betrayed. أَكاذِيب

husbandmen farmers or people who cultivate the land, especially in the context of traditional agriculture.
Farmers, cultivators, tillers, agriculturists, growers.   The husbandmen worked tirelessly from dawn to dusk, ensuring that their crops were well-tended and their livestock healthy. فَلَّاحون

iconoclast a person who attacks or criticizes cherished beliefs or institutions. In historical contexts, it refers to someone who destroys religious images or opposes their veneration. Dissenter, nonconformist, rebel, skeptic, critic. The young artist was seen as an iconoclast for challenging the traditional conventions of the art world. مُحَطِّم الأَيقونَات

ignoble actions or character traits that are not honorable in character or purpose; of low birth or common origin. Dishonorable, base, shameful, despicable, sordid. His ignoble actions during the competition, such as cheating and lying, tarnished his reputation. دَنِيء

ignominy public shame or disgrace. Shame, disgrace, dishonor, humiliation, embarrassment. The politician faced ignominy after the scandal was exposed, leading to his resignation. عار

ill-disposed having a negative or hostile attitude towards someone or something. Hostile, unfriendly, antagonistic, inimical, unsympathetic. He was ill-disposed towards the new policies, believing they would harm the community. سَيِّئُ الذَرِّيَّة

imbibe to drink, especially alcohol. It can also mean to absorb or assimilate ideas or knowledge. Drink, consume, quaff, absorb, assimilate. The students were eager to imbibe the wisdom of their experienced professor during the lecture. يَرْتَشِف

imbibed	to have drunk, especially alcohol. It can also mean to have absorbed or assimilated ideas or knowledge.	Drank, consumed, quaffed, absorbed, assimilated.	She imbibed the culture and traditions of the country during her year abroad. اِرْتَشَفَ

imbibement	the act of drinking, especially alcohol, or the absorption or assimilation of ideas or knowledge.	Drinking, consumption, absorption, assimilation, intake. The evening was filled with merriment and imbibement as friends gathered to celebrate the holiday season. اِرْتِشاف

imbrued	to stain or soak, especially with blood.	Stained, soaked, drenched, tainted, sullied. The battlefield was imbrued with the blood of countless soldiers. مُلَطَّخ

imbue	to inspire or permeate with a feeling or quality.	Infuse, instill, inspire, permeate, saturate.	The teacher aimed to imbue her students with a love of learning and curiosity about the world. يَغْمُر

immaculate	perfectly clean, neat, or tidy; free from flaws or mistakes.	Spotless, pristine, flawless, unblemished, pure.	The house was immaculate after the cleaning crew finished their work, with every surface shining and no clutter in sight. نَقِّي

immoderacy	the quality of being excessive or lacking in moderation. Excessiveness, intemperance, overindulgence, extremeness, extravagance.	His immoderacy in spending led to financial troubles and debt. إِفْراط

immolation   the act of killing or offering as a sacrifice, especially by burning. Sacrifice, offering, oblation, burning, martyrdom.   The ancient ritual involved the immolation of a lamb to appease the gods. تَضْحِيَة

impart   to make information known; to communicate or pass on knowledge, wisdom, or information. Communicate, convey, transmit, share, disclose.   Arab alchemists imparted therapeutic values to precious stones.   يُقْضِي-حَمَل

impasse   a situation in which no progress is possible, especially because of disagreement; a deadlock.   Deadlock, stalemate, standstill, standoff, gridlock.   The negotiations reached an impasse when neither side could agree on the terms of the contract. طَرِيق مَسْدُود

impeach   to charge (a holder of public office) with misconduct, especially to accuse a public official of a crime or misconduct in office. Accuse, charge, indict, prosecute, denounce. The congress voted to impeach the president for alleged abuses of power and obstruction of justice. يَعْزِل

impede   to delay or prevent someone or something by obstructing them; hinder.   Hinder, obstruct, hamper, block, delay.   The heavy snowfall impeded the progress of the rescue mission, making it difficult for the team to reach the stranded hikers. يُعَرْقِل

impediment   something that makes it difficult to do or complete something; an obstacle or hindrance.

Obstacle, hindrance, barrier, obstruction, drawback.   His speech impediment made public speaking a challenge, but he worked hard to overcome it.   عائِق

impingement   the action or process of interfering or having an effect, often in a negative or intrusive way.

Intrusion, encroachment, impact, interference, infringement.   The constant noise from the construction site was an impingement on the residents' daily lives.   تَدَخُّل

imperceptible   so slight, gradual, or subtle as not to be perceived.   Unnoticeable, undetectable, faint, subtle, indistinguishable.   The changes in the landscape were imperceptible at first, only becoming noticeable after several years.   غَيْر مَلْمُوس

impermanence   the state or fact of lasting for only a limited period; transience.   Transience, temporariness, fleetingness, ephemerality, instability.

The impermanence of life is a central theme in many philosophical and religious traditions, reminding us to appreciate each moment.   زَوَال

impertinence   lack of respect or rudeness; inappropriate or bold behavior or speech.   Rudeness, insolence, disrespect, impudence, cheekiness.
The student's impertinence towards the teacher earned him a reprimand and detention.   وَقاحَة

impertinent   being rude or showing a lack of respect; not pertinent or relevant to a particular matter.
Rude, insolent, disrespectful, impudent, cheeky.
The impertinent comment during the meeting offended several colleagues.   وَقِح

impervious   not allowing fluid to pass through or unable to be affected by something. Impenetrable, impermeable, resistant, unaffected, invulnerable.   The new raincoat is made of a material that is impervious to water, keeping the wearer dry even in heavy downpours.   مُضادّ لِلتّسَرُّب-حَصِين

impetuous   acting or done quickly and without thought or care; moving forcefully or rapidly. Rash, hasty, impulsive, reckless, spontaneous.   His impetuous decision to quit his job without a backup plan left him struggling financially. مُتَهَوِّر

impetus   the force or energy with which a body moves; something that makes a process or activity happen or happen more quickly.   Motivation, drive, stimulus, incentive, momentum.   The new policy provided fresh impetus for economic growth in the region. دافِع

implode   to collapse or cause to collapse violently inward.Collapse, cave in, fall in, crumple, burst inward.   The old building imploded in a cloud of dust as the demolition team triggered the explosives.
يَنْفَجِر داخِلِيّاً

importune   to ask someone persistently for or to do something.   Beg, beseech, implore, solicit, entreat.

The salesman continued to importune customers, despite their clear lack of interest in his product. يُلِحّ

importunity   persistent and insistent demands or requests, often to the point of being annoying or intrusive.   Persistence, insistence, pestering, nagging, badgering.   Her importunity in asking for a raise annoyed her boss, who felt pressured to respond. إلْحاح

impracticable   not capable of being put into practice or carried out; not feasible or practical.   Infeasible, unworkable, impossible, unrealistic, unattainable.
Given the time constraints, the original plan proved impracticable, so they had to come up with an alternative solution. غَيْر عَمَلِي

inadmissible not allowed or considered acceptable, especially in a court of law due to being improper or not meeting legal standards.   Unacceptable, inadmissible, barred, prohibited, not permissible.   The judge ruled the evidence as inadmissible because it was obtained illegally. غَيْر قابِل للقَبول-مرفوض

inaptitude   a lack of skill or ability for a particular task or job; incompetence.   Incompetence, incapacity, ineptitude, unfitness, inability. His inaptitude for public speaking made him nervous and ineffective during presentations. عَدَم الكَفاءة

inauguration   the formal ceremony or process of starting something new or the formal introduction into office or position.   Induction, initiation, installation, commencement, swearing-in. The president's inauguration was attended by thousands of people who gathered to witness the historic event.   دَنصيب

inauspicious   describes something that is not likely to bring success or favorable outcomes; unfavorable or unlucky.   Unfavorable, unfortunate, unlucky, ominous, adverse.   The stormy weather on the day of their wedding was seen as an inauspicious start to their marriage.   غَير مُحَظّى بِه، غَير مُبَشّر

incapacitated   to be deprived of strength or ability; unable to function normally due to physical or mental impairment.   Disabled, impaired, debilitated, incapacitated, paralyzed.   After the accident, he was incapacitated and unable to work for several months.   مُعَاق-عاجِز

incensed   extremely angry; enraged.   Furious, enraged, infuriated, outraged, incensed.   The community was incensed by the unjust decision of the city council.   غاضِب جِدّاً

incessant   describes something that continues without interruption; constant or unceasing.   Continuous, uninterrupted, constant, relentless, perpetual.   The incessant noise of the construction site made it difficult to concentrate.   مُتَواصِل

incommensurable   refers to things that are not able to be compared or measured against each other because they are fundamentally different in nature or scale. Incomparable, incomputable, immeasurable, unmeasurable, unquantifiable.   The beauty of the artwork and the complexity of the scientific theory were incommensurable, making it challenging to judge which was more valuable. غَيْر قابِل للمُقارَدَة-ممتنع المقايسة

incommensurate   not in proportion or corresponding in degree or amount; disproportionate or inadequate.   Disproportionate, unequal, inadequate, insufficient, disproportionate. His salary was incommensurate with his qualifications and experience, leading to dissatisfaction with his job.   غَيْر مُتَناسِب-
غير متقايس

incongruity   the state of being incongruous, or lacking harmony, consistency, or compatibility between different things. Inconsistency, discrepancy, disparity, discordance, mismatch.   The incongruity between his actions and his words puzzled his friends, who couldn't understand his behavior.   عَدَم التَّدَاسُق

inconsequential   not important or significant; lacking relevance or importance.   Trivial, minor, insignificant, unimportant, negligible.   The small mistakes he made were inconsequential in the grand scheme of the project.   تافِه

inconsolable   describes someone who cannot be comforted or consoled, often due to grief, sorrow, or distress.   Distraught, devastated, desolate, heartbroken, grief-stricken.   She was inconsolable after the loss of her beloved pet cat. لا يُمكِن تَعويضه-لا
عزاء له

incorrigible   describes a person who is beyond correction, reform, or improvement, especially in behavior. Unmanageable, unruly, uncontrollable, irredeemable, hopeless. Despite numerous attempts at rehabilitation, he remained incorrigible and continued to engage in criminal activities. لا يُقَدَّر على إصْلاحِه-عَنِيد

incredulity the state of being unwilling or unable to believe something; skepticism or disbelief. Disbelief, skepticism, doubt, suspicion, mistrust. His story was met with incredulity by everyone present, as it seemed too fantastical to be true. شكوكِيّة-ارتِيَاب

incredulous someone who is unwilling or unable to believe something; skeptical or disbelieving. Skeptical, doubtful, dubious, suspicious, wary. She gave him an incredulous look when he told her he had won the lottery. مُشَكِّك

incriminate to accuse or implicate someone in a crime or wrongdoing. Accuse, charge, indict, implicate, blame. The evidence found at the scene was enough to incriminate the suspect in the theft. يُتَّهَم-اجتَرَم

incriminatory something that suggests or serves as evidence of guilt or involvement in a crime or wrongdoing. Damning, accusatory, indicting, condemning, inculpatory. The incriminatory documents found in his possession linked him directly to the illegal activities. مُحَمِّل بِالتَّهْمَة-تجريمي

incumbent 1. someone who currently holds a particular office or position, especially in politics or business. 2. It can also mean necessary as a duty or responsibility. 1. Officeholder, official, holder, occupant. 2. Mandatory, obligatory, necessary, required.   1. The incumbent mayor is running for reelection this year. 2. It is incumbent upon all citizens to vote in the upcoming election.   المتربّع (للحامل لمنصب)-إلزاميّ-ضَرُورِي

incur to become subject to (something unwelcome or unpleasant) as a result of one's own behavior or actions.   Suffer, experience, face, undergo, bear.   He incurred heavy losses in the stock market due to risky investments.   يُكبِد-يَتَعَرَّض ُ ل

incursion   a sudden and usually unwelcome invasion or attack into a territory or area, especially by armed forces.   Invasion, raid, attack, assault, foray.   The army launched an incursion into enemy territory under the cover of darkness.غَزْو-غَارَة-هَجْوم

indelible   something that cannot be removed, forgotten, or erased; permanent or lasting.   Permanent, lasting, enduring, ingrained, unforgettable.   The experience left an indelible mark on her memory, shaping her views for years to come.لا يُمكن محوه-دائِم

indemnification   the act of compensating someone for harm or loss incurred, often through insurance or legal means.   Compensation, reimbursement, repayment, restitution, reparation.   The contract included an indemnification clause that protected the company against financial losses resulting from legal disputes.   تَعويض

indentured-servant a laborer under contract to work for someone for a specific period of time, often to pay off a debt or to learn a trade or skill. articled servant, bondslave, bondsman.   The outline represents Grace Wisher, a free Black child who was Pickersgill's indentured servant and apprentice. عمال السخرة-خدم بقيد- أجير

indictment   a formal accusation or charge of a serious crime, typically presented by a grand jury and usually leading to trial.   Accusation, charge, allegation, prosecution, summons.   The grand jury returned an indictment against the suspect for multiple counts of fraud and embezzlement. لائِحَة اتّهام

indigence   extreme poverty or a state of being extremely poor and lacking basic necessities.   Poverty, destitution, neediness, penury, impoverishment.   The charity organization aimed to alleviate the indigence of families living in the slums by providing food and shelter. فَقْر

indignant   feeling or showing anger or annoyance at what is perceived as unfair treatment or injustice.   Angry, furious, incensed, outraged, irate.   She was indignant at being accused of something she didn't do. غاضِب-ساخِط

indignation   strong displeasure at something considered unjust, offensive, or insulting; righteous anger. Anger, resentment, fury, wrath, ire.   Her indignation was evident when she learned about the company's discriminatory hiring practices. غَضَب-سُخْط

indite   write or compose, especially literary or formal writing. Write, compose, pen, draft, scribble. The poet

indited a beautiful sonnet in honor of his beloved.
كَتَبَ-ألْفى

indivisible   unable to be divided or separated into parts; not divisible.   Inseparable, unbreakable, whole, unified, undivided.   The bond between the two sisters was so strong that they considered themselves indivisible.   لا يُقَسَّم-غَيْر قابِل للتَّقْسِيم

inducement   something that persuades or influences someone to do something, typically by offering an incentive or motivation.   Incentive, motivation, encouragement, stimulus, enticement.   The signing bonus served as a strong inducement for the talented recruit to join the company.   حافِز-اِسْتِمَالَة

inebriated   to be affected by alcohol to the extent of losing control of one's faculties or behaviors; drunk.   Drunk, intoxicated, intoxicated, tipsy, under the influence.   He became inebriated after drinking several glasses of wine at the party.   مُسْكِر-مَخْمُور

ineffable   describes something that is too great or extreme to be expressed or described in words; beyond description.   Indescribable, inexpressible, unimaginable, transcendent, beyond words.   The beauty of the sunrise over the mountains left them with an ineffable sense of awe.   لا يُوصَف-فائِق الوصف

ineffectually without producing the desired effect; ineffectively.   Inefficiently, ineffectively, unsuccessfully, ineptly, futilely.   Despite his efforts, he acted ineffectually in resolving the ongoing conflict.   دون جِدوى

ineptitude   a lack of skill or ability, especially in a particular activity or job; incompetence.
Incompetence, incapacity, clumsiness, awkwardness, ineffectiveness.   His ineptitude in handling customer complaints led to a decline in customer satisfaction. عَدَم الكَفاءة

infamy   refers to being well known for a bad quality or deed; the state of being infamous or having a notorious reputation.   Notoriety, disgrace, dishonor, shame, ignominy.   The dictator's infamy spread throughout the world due to his brutal regime and human rights abuses.   العار-سُمْعَة سَيِّئَة

infanticide   the act of killing an infant, especially shortly after birth.   Child murder, neonaticide, filicide.   Infanticide is a tragic and criminal act that is universally condemned.   قَتْل الرُّضَّع

infirmity   a physical or mental weakness or ailment, especially one that is chronic or related to old age.   Weakness, ailment, illness, disability, debility.   Despite her physical infirmities, she remained mentally sharp and active in her community. عُجز-ضَعَف

ingenuousness   the quality of being innocent, frank, and straightforward; lacking in cunning or deceit.   Sincerity, honesty, openness, simplicity, candidness.   His ingenuousness in sharing his personal experiences made him a trustworthy friend.   صِدَق-بَرَاءَة

ingrate   someone who is ungrateful or fails to acknowledge kindness or benefits received from others.   Ungrateful person, thankless individual, unappreciative person.   Despite all that she did for him, he turned out to be an ingrate, never showing any appreciation. غَيْر مُمْدَّن-عاق

ingratiating   describes behavior that is intended to gain favor or approval, often by being charming, flattering, or pleasing. Flattering, charming, flattering, pleasing, obsequious. She adopted an ingratiating demeanor during the job interview to impress the interviewers. مُسْتَرْضٍ-تَزَلّف-مُتَمَلِّق

inhibition   a feeling of self-consciousness or a constraint in one's behavior, actions, or emotions.   Restraint, hesitation, reservation, constraint, inhibition.   His shyness and inhibition prevented him from speaking up during the meeting.   تَثْبِيط

inhibitory   refers to something that has the effect of inhibiting or restraining action, process, or function.   Restrictive, restraining, inhibiting, controlling, suppressive.   The drug has an inhibitory effect on the growth of bacteria.   مُثَبِّط

inhospitably   describes an unwelcoming or unfriendly manner, especially in terms of the treatment of guests or visitors.   Unwelcoming, unfriendly, hostile, coldly, harshly.   Despite their reputation for hospitality, they treated us inhospitably during our stay.
بِطريقة غَيْر حَسَنة-بلا حفاوة

inimical harmful or adverse, especially in effect; tending to obstruct or harm. Harmful, detrimental, hostile, unfriendly, adverse. The new regulations proved inimical to small businesses, causing many to struggle to stay afloat. مُضِرّ

iniquitous something that is grossly unfair or morally wrong; characterized by injustice or wickedness. Unjust, immoral, wicked, sinful, evil. The ruler's iniquitous actions led to widespread suffering and discontent among the population. ظالم-فاسِق

injudicious lacking good judgment or discretion; unwise or imprudent. Unwise, imprudent, foolish, ill-advised, reckless. His injudicious remarks during the meeting offended many colleagues and jeopardized team harmony. غَيْر حكيم

injurious describes something that causes harm or damage, especially physically or morally. Harmful, damaging, detrimental, hurtful, destructive. Smoking is known to have injurious effects on both the smoker's health and those around them. مؤذٍ

innocuous not harmful or offensive; unlikely to cause harm or injury. Harmless, benign, safe, non-threatening, mild. The spider in the corner of the room looked innocuous, but she still called for someone to remove it. غَيْر ضارّ-حميد

inoculate to treat with a vaccine to produce immunity against a disease; to introduce a microorganism into a culture medium. Vaccinate, immunize, protect, safeguard. The healthcare

workers will inoculate children against measles during
the vaccination campaign.   يُطْعِم-يُحَصِّن

inscrutable   describes something that is mysterious,
difficult to understand, or not easily interpreted or
understood.   Mysterious, enigmatic, obscure,
incomprehensible, unfathomable.   His inscrutable
expression made it hard for others to gauge his true
feelings.   غامِض-مُبهَم

insidious   something that proceeds in a gradual,
subtle way, but with harmful effects that are often
unnoticed until it is too late.   Stealthy, cunning,
treacherous, deceitful, sneaky.   The disease had
an insidious onset, with symptoms appearing slowly
over time.   خبيث-ماكِر

insubordinate   a person who refuses to obey
orders from someone in authority, or who shows a lack
of respect for authority.   Disobedient, defiant,
rebellious, unruly, recalcitrant.   The employee was
fired for being consistently insubordinate towards their
supervisor.   مُتَمَرِّد-عاص

insuperable   something that cannot be overcome or
dealt with successfully; impossible to overcome.
      Insurmountable, unbeatable, impassable,
overwhelming, invincible.   The challenges they faced
seemed insuperable at first, but they eventually found a
way to overcome them.   لا يُتَغَلَّب عليه-لا يُتَحَدّى

intercalary   something inserted or introduced
between others that are regular or usual, often referring
to an inserted day in a calendar.   Inserted,

supplementary, additional, extra.   The intercalary month was added to synchronize the lunar calendar with the solar year.   و سَيط-كبيس

interpretive   relates to the act or process of explaining or interpreting something, especially a text or artwork, in order to understand its meaning or significance. Explanatory, explanatory, elucidatory, illustrative.   The interpretive dance performance conveyed deep emotions through movement and expression.
تَفْسِيرِي

intuited   is the past tense of the verb "intuit," which means to understand or know something without the need for conscious reasoning; to grasp or perceive something instinctively.   Perceived, sensed, apprehended, understood, realized. She intuited that something was wrong when he didn't show up for their meeting.   حدس

inundate   overwhelm someone or something with a large amount of things or people, often causing problems.   Overwhelm, flood, swamp, deluge, engulf. The company was inundated with job applications after posting the vacancy online.
غَمَر-غَرَق

inured   to become accustomed to something unpleasant or difficult over time, such that it no longer affects one deeply.   Accustomed, habituated, desensitized, toughened, hardened. Having worked in the emergency room for years, she had become inured to the sight of blood and injuries.   تأقلم-مُمَرَّس

invasive something that intrudes or spreads aggressively, especially where it is not wanted or harmful to the environment or health. Intrusive, encroaching, invasive, penetrating, trespassing. The invasive species of plants were rapidly taking over the native habitat, threatening local biodiversity. غَزوي-اجتياحي

invective refers to abusive language used to express blame, censure, or bitter deep-seated ill will. Abuse, vituperation, denunciation, diatribe, tirade. His speech was filled with invective against his political opponents, accusing them of corruption and dishonesty. ٱنتِقاد لاذِع-ذَمّي

inveighed is the past tense of the verb "inveigh," which means to speak or write about something with great hostility or strong protest. Rail against, protest strongly, condemn, denounce, criticize vehemently. She inveighed against the government's decision to cut funding for public schools during her speech. انتقد بشدة-هاجم بعنف

inveterate describes a habit, feeling, or behavior that is long-established and unlikely to change. Chronic, entrenched, habitual, persistent, deep-rooted. He was an inveterate smoker, having smoked a pack a day for over thirty years. مُتأصِّرّل-مُعتاد

irradiate 1. To expose to radiation, such as light or heat. 2. To illuminate or light up. 3. To treat with radiation for medical purposes. 1. Illuminate, light up, shine on. 2. Radiate, emit, beam. 3. Treat, expose, subject. 1. The sun irradiates the Earth with light and heat. 2. Her face irradiated with joy when she saw the surprise. 3. The patient was irradiated with high-energy beams to target the tumor.   يُشِعّ-يُنَير

irresolute   describes someone who is uncertain or hesitant; lacking in firmness of purpose or determination. Indecisive, hesitant, unsure, vacillating, wavering.   His irresolute behavior made it difficult for the team to make progress on the project.
مُتَرَدِّد-غَير حاسِم

irreverence   a lack of respect for people or things that are generally taken seriously or considered sacred.   Disrespect, contempt, disdain, disregard, sacrilege.   His irreverence towards authority figures often led to conflicts in the workplace.
استخفاف-عدم الاحترام

irrevocable   describes something that cannot be changed, reversed, or undone; final and irreversible.   Unalterable, irreversible, permanent, final, fixed.   Signing the contract meant making an irrevocable commitment to the terms agreed upon.   لا رَجْعة فيه

isthmus   a narrow strip of land with water on both sides, connecting two larger land areas.   Neck, neck of land, strip of land, narrow land bridge.   The Panama Canal cuts through the isthmus connecting North and South America, providing a vital shipping route.   نِطاق-بَرزَخ-حاجِز

itinerary   a detailed plan or route of a journey or travel, including destinations, dates, and times.

Schedule, agenda, route, program, travel plan.
They prepared a detailed itinerary for their vacation, including flights, accommodations, and sightseeing activities. جَدول سَفَر

ivory   the hard, creamy-white substance composing the tusks of elephants, walruses, and other animals.
Tusk, bone, tooth, white.   The trade of ivory has been heavily regulated due to its association with the illegal poaching of elephants.   عاج

J j

jeered   is the past tense of the verb "jeer," which means to make rude and mocking remarks or sounds to express scorn or ridicule.   Mocked, taunted, scoffed, derided, teased.   The crowd jeered at the opposing team's player after he missed the crucial penalty kick. ‎هَدَّفَ-سـدخَر‎

jesuit   a member of the Society of Jesus, a Roman Catholic religious order known for its educational, missionary, and charitable works.   The Jesuit priest dedicated his life to teaching and serving communities in need around the world.   The Jesuit priest dedicated his life to teaching and serving communities in need around the world.   ‎يسوعي‎

jiffy   a very short period of time; a moment or instant.   Moment, instant, second, twinkling, flash.   She'll be ready in a jiffy; she just needs to finish her makeup.   ‎لحظة-لَمْح البَصرَ‎

jiggered   1. Used to express surprise, dismay, or annoyance. 2. totally damaged. 3. a type of measurement tool or device used for pouring precise amounts of liquid, typically in bartending.   1. Surprised, dismayed, annoyed (informal usage). 2. defective, damaged, broken. 3. Measure, tool, device (nautical and engineering context).   1. "Well, I'll be jiggered! I didn't expect to see you here." 2. the lens is totally jiggered. 3. The bartender used a jiggered to pour precise amounts of whiskey for the cocktails.

‎مندهش-أداة غِربال- يعاني من خلل او عطل‎

jocose   playful or humorous in a light-hearted way; characterized by joking or jesting.   Jocular, witty, humorous, playful, jovial.   His jocose nature made him popular at social gatherings, always ready with a witty remark or joke.   مُفَرِّح-مُسَلِّ

jocularity   the quality or state of being jocular; characterized by joking or humor.   Humor, wit, jesting, merriment, fun.   The dinner party was filled with laughter and jocularity, creating a lively and enjoyable atmosphere.   مَرَح-دِعابَة

jostle to push, elbow, or bump against someone or something forcefully, typically in a crowded place.   Push, shove, elbow, crowd, jolt.   The commuters jostled each other as they hurried to catch the train during rush hour.   تَدافُع

jurisprudence   the theory or philosophy of law, or the study and interpretation of legal principles and rules.   Legal theory, law philosophy, legal system, legal science.   His deep understanding of jurisprudence allowed him to argue complex legal cases with clarity and precision.   الفَلْسَفَة القانونِيَّة

K k L l

klutz   a clumsy or awkward person who tends to frequently drop or break things.   Clumsy person, oaf, bungler, butterfingers.   Despite his best efforts, he couldn't help but feel like a klutz whenever he tried to dance. غبيّ-أخرق

lackadaisical   someone who lacks enthusiasm, determination, or effort; lazy or indifferent.   Indifferent, lazy, apathetic, sluggish, lethargic.   His lackadaisical approach to studying resulted in poor grades at the end of the semester.   غَيْر مُبالٍ-رَخو

lackey   a servant, especially a liveried footman or manservant; also used figuratively to describe someone who behaves in a servile or submissive way.
      Servant, attendant, minion, follower, henchman.
      The wealthy merchant's lackey carried his bags and attended to his every need.   خادِم-مُتَصَنِّع

laconic   a style of speech or writing that uses few words, often to the point of being terse or concise.
      Brief, concise, succinct, terse, to the point.   His laconic response to the interviewer's questions left them wanting more details. مُخْتَصَر

lacuna   a gap or missing part, especially in a manuscript or a literary work, where something is absent or omitted.   Gap, hiatus, blank, missing part, deficiency.   The historian discovered a lacuna in the ancient text where several pages had been lost over time. فَجْوة-نَقْص

lampoonery   the act of writing or creating satire, mocking, or ridiculing someone or something in a humorous or sarcastic way.   Satire, mockery, ridicule, parody, spoof. His lampoonery of political figures in his comedy sketches often drew both laughter and criticism. سُخْرِيَّة-هُزْل

languor   a state of tiredness or inertia, often characterized by a lack of energy or interest.   Lethargy, listlessness, sluggishness, weariness, apathy.   The heat of the afternoon induced a sense of languor in the sleepy town. كَسَل-خَمَول

Larceny   the unlawful taking and carrying away of someone else's personal property with the intent to deprive the owner of it permanently. Theft, stealing, robbery, pilfering, thievery.   He was arrested and charged with larceny after stealing a valuable painting from the art gallery. سَرِقة

latent   describes something that exists but is not yet developed, visible, or active; potentially existing but not presently evident or realized. Dormant, potential, hidden, concealed, undeveloped.   Her latent artistic talent emerged when she started painting in her late twenties.   كامِن-مُخْفَى

latitude   1. the distance north or south of the equator, measured in degrees,. 2. freedom from restriction; the scope for freedom of action or thought.   1. Longitude, parallels, tropic, Arctic Circle, Antarctic Circle, polar. 2. leeway, freedom, liberty, scope, room.   1. The latitude of Cairo is approximately

30 degrees north. 2. They were given considerable latitude in how they conducted their research.   خَطّ
عُرُض-دُرِّيّة

laureate   someone who has been honored or awarded a prize for outstanding achievement, especially in literature, art, or science. It can also refer to a person who has been crowned with a laurel wreath as a symbol of victory or honor in ancient times.
    Prizewinner, award winner, Nobel laureate, victor.   The poet was named the poet laureate of the country for his contributions to literature.   حائز على
جائزة-فائز

lavatory   a room equipped with a toilet and sink, primarily used for personal hygiene purposes.
    Restroom, bathroom, toilet, washroom, powder room. After a long flight, she was relieved to find a clean lavatory in the airport where she could freshen up.
    مِرْحَاض

laving the act of washing or bathing, often used in a more poetic or literary context.   Washing, bathing, cleansing, rinsing, ablution.   The gentle stream was perfect for laving her tired feet after a long hike.
    اِغْتِسَال

layoff temporary or permanent termination of employment by an employer, often due to financial reasons or restructuring.   Dismissal, discharge, redundancy, furlough, termination.   The company announced a massive layoff due to declining sales, affecting hundreds of employees.   فَصْل عَن العَمَل

leaden   heavy and slow, resembling the weight and dullness of lead; it can also describe a dull, gray color or a sluggish, depressed mood. Heavy, sluggish, dull, burdensome, gray.   After the long and exhausting meeting, she felt a leaden weariness settle over her.
ثَقِيل كَالرَّصَاص-كئيب

lecherous   describes someone who shows excessive or offensive sexual desire. Lustful, lascivious, licentious, salacious, lewd.   The character in the novel was portrayed as a lecherous old man, constantly making inappropriate remarks to the women around him.   شَهْوَانِي

legate   an official representative or envoy, often sent on a special diplomatic mission or to represent the interests of an organization.   Envoy, ambassador, emissary, delegate, representative.   The Pope sent a trusted legate to negotiate peace between the warring nations.   مَبْعُوث

leitmotif   a recurring theme or idea in a piece of music, literature, or art that is associated with a particular person, idea, or situation.   Theme, motif, recurrent theme, idea, subject.   In the symphony, the composer used a haunting melody as a leitmotif to represent the protagonist's struggle.   لَحْن مُتَكَرِّر-نزعات متكررة

leniency   the quality of being more merciful or tolerant than expected; it involves showing clemency or forgiveness in judgment or punishment.   Mercy, clemency, tolerance, compassion, forgiveness.   The judge showed leniency towards the first-time offender,

opting for community service instead of jail time.
تَسَاهُل-رَحمَة-رَأفَة

lenient   someone who is permissive, merciful, or tolerant, often showing more forgiveness or flexibility than is typical. Merciful, tolerant, forgiving, compassionate, indulgent.   The teacher was lenient with the students who missed the deadline, giving them an extra week to complete their assignments.
مُتَسَاهِل-رَحِيم-عَطُوف

lesion   any damage or abnormal change in the tissue of an organism, usually caused by disease or trauma.   Wound, injury, sore, ulcer, abrasion.   The doctor examined the lesion on her skin to determine if it was benign or required further treatment.   آفَة

lest   a conjunction used to introduce a clause expressing fear or precaution to avoid a negative outcome.   In case, for fear that, so that ... not, to prevent, to avoid.   She spoke quietly, lest she wake the sleeping baby.   خَشْيَةَ أن

lethargy   a state of sluggishness, inactivity, and apathy, often characterized by a lack of energy or enthusiasm.   Sluggishness, inactivity, apathy, lassitude, torpor.   After recovering from the flu, he still felt a lingering lethargy that made it difficult to resume his daily activities.   خُمُول

levied   imposed or collected, typically referring to taxes, fees, or fines by an authority. Imposed, charged, assessed, collected, exacted. The government levied a

new tax on luxury goods to increase revenue.
فَرَضَ

levy   the act of imposing or collecting a tax, fee, or fine, or it can refer to the amount that is collected.   Tax, fee, charge, duty, tariff.   The city council decided to impose a levy on all commercial properties to fund public transportation improvements. ضَرِيبَة-إِتَاوَة-كَلَّف-
فرض

liaison   a person who acts as a link to assist communication or cooperation between groups of people, or the communication and cooperation itself.   Link, intermediary, mediator, connection, coordinator.   She served as a liaison between the two departments, ensuring that information flowed smoothly and projects stayed on track. رَابِطَة-آصِرَة

lice   small, wingless, parasitic insects that live on the skin of mammals and birds, feeding on their blood.   Parasites, nits, cooties, bugs, pests.   The school conducted regular checks to prevent the spread of lice among students.   قَمْل

licentious   behavior that is unrestrained by law or morality, often in a sexual context.   Immoral, lewd, lascivious, debauched, dissolute.   The novel's protagonist was criticized for her licentious lifestyle, which defied the strict social norms of her time.   فَاجِر

lien   a legal claim or right against a property that allows the holder to obtain access to the property if debts are not paid.   Claim, charge, encumbrance, mortgage, security interest.   The bank placed a lien on the house until the mortgage was fully paid off. رَهْن

lieu   place or stead; it is often used in the phrase "in lieu of," meaning instead of or in place of.   Instead of, in place of, as a substitute for, as an alternative to, rather than.   He opted to take a day off in lieu of extra pay for working on the holiday. بِدَلاً مِن

limekiln   a kiln or furnace used for burning limestone or shells to produce lime, a material used in construction, agriculture, and various industrial processes.   Lime furnace, lime oven, kiln, lime burner, calciner.   The old limekiln, once crucial for producing building materials, now stood abandoned on the edge of town.   فُرْن الجِير

limelight   the focus of public attention or the center of interest and acclaim.   Spotlight, attention, prominence, public eye, center stage.   After winning the award, she found herself in the limelight, receiving praise and attention from the media.
الأَضْوَاء-بريق الشهرة

linchpin   a central, cohesive element that holds various parts together, often used metaphorically to describe someone or something essential to the functioning of an organization or system.   Keystone, cornerstone, foundation, mainstay, anchor. Her expertise and leadership were the linchpin of the project, ensuring its successful completion. عُنْصُر
أَسَاسِي

lineament   a distinctive feature or characteristic, especially of the face. It can also refer to an outline or contour of a figure.   Feature, characteristic, contour, profile, trait.   The artist captured every lineament of her face, highlighting the delicate features that made her unique. ملامح-مَعَالِم

lionize   to treat someone as a very important or famous person, often giving them a lot of public attention and admiration.   Glorify, idolize, celebrate, praise, exalt.   The community lionized the young athlete after she brought home the gold medal, celebrating her achievements with a grand parade. يُمَجِّد-يُعَظِّم

litanies   repetitive or lengthy lists or recitals, often referring to a form of prayer involving a series of invocations and responses.   Chants, recitals, prayers, invocations, supplications.   During the ceremony, the congregation recited the litanies with solemn devotion, each phrase echoing through the church.   أَدْعِيَة مُتَكَرِّرَة-اِبتهالات

lithe   someone who is thin, supple, and graceful in movement.   Supple, agile, graceful, limber, flexible.   The dancer's lithe movements captivated the audience, showcasing her incredible flexibility and control.   رَشِيق

liturgy   a prescribed form or set of forms for public religious worship, especially in Christian services.   Ritual, ceremony, worship, service, rite.   The church's liturgy has remained unchanged for centuries, providing a sense of continuity and tradition for its congregation. طُقُوس دِينِيَّة-شَعِيرَة-قدّاس

livery   a distinctive uniform worn by servants or officials, or the distinctive colors and designs associated with a particular group, company, or individual, especially as seen on vehicles.   Uniform, attire, costume, regalia, insignia.   The hotel staff wore a smart livery that matched the elegant decor of the establishment. زِيّ رَسْمِي

locomotion   the act or ability of moving from one place to another, often referring to the movement of living organisms or vehicles. Movement, motion, mobility, transit, travel.   The study of animal locomotion provides insights into how different species have adapted to their environments. حَرَكَة-اِنتِقال

locus a particular position, point, or place, often used in mathematical or scientific contexts to describe a specific location of points that satisfy a certain condition.   Location, site, position, spot, place.   it is impossible to specify the exact locus in the brain of these neural events   مَوْقِع

loll   to sit, lie, or stand in a lazy, relaxed way, often with limbs flopped loosely or hanging down.   Lounge, sprawl, laze, recline, slump.   On the hot summer afternoon, he liked to loll on the porch, sipping lemonade and watching the clouds drift by.   يَسْتَرْخِي- تَدَلَّى

lopsided   uneven or crooked, with one side lower or smaller than the other, giving an appearance of imbalance.   Uneven, asymmetrical, unbalanced, skewed, tilted.   The table had a lopsided appearance because one of its legs was shorter than the others. غَيْر مُتَوَازِن

loquacious   describes someone who is very talkative, often to an excessive degree. Talkative, chatty, garrulous, verbose, voluble.   Her loquacious nature made her popular at parties, where she could always be found engaging others in lively conversation. ثَرْثَار

lota   a small, usually spherical water vessel, commonly used in South Asian countries for personal hygiene and religious rituals. Water pot, pitcher, vessel, container, ewer.   In the early morning, she filled the lota with water from the well to prepare for her daily prayers.   إِبْرِيق

lucidity   the quality of being easily understood, completely intelligible, or comprehensible; it also describes a state of clarity of thought or mind.   Clarity, clearness, intelligibility, transparency, explicitness.   The professor's lucidity in explaining complex theories made the lecture enjoyable and informative for all the students.   وُضُوح

luminaries   people who inspire or influence others, especially those who are prominent in a particular sphere; it can also refer to natural light-giving bodies like the sun or moon. Influencers, leaders, celebrities, notables, icons.   The conference was attended by many luminaries in the field of science, each sharing their groundbreaking research.   مَشاهير - أَعلام

luster   a gentle sheen or soft glow, especially that of a partly reflective surface. It can also describe a quality that outshines the usual, providing radiance and brilliance.   Shine, sheen, gloss, radiance, brilliance.   The antique vase had lost its luster over the years, but it still held a certain charm and elegance. بَريق

lynching   the illegal execution of someone, typically by a mob, often by hanging, without a legal trial, usually motivated by racial prejudice or perceived crimes.Mob justice, execution, hanging, murder, vigilantism.   The tragic history of lynching in the United States is a somber reminder of the consequences of racial hatred and injustice.
إعْدام غَيْر قَاذُونِيّ-اعدام دون محاكمة

M m

machination   a plot or scheme, typically one that is cunning, crafty, or deceitful.   Scheme, plot, conspiracy, intrigue, stratagem.   The villain's machination to overthrow the government was foiled by the vigilant intelligence agency.   مُؤَامَرَة-مَكِيدَة

magistrat   a civil officer or judge who administers the law, especially one who conducts minor offenses and preliminary hearings.   Judge, justice, adjudicator, official, arbiter.   The magistrate listened carefully to both sides before making a fair and just decision.   قَاضٍ

magnitude   the great size, extent, or importance of something. In a scientific context, it can also refer to the measure of an earthquake's strength or the brightness of a star.   Size, extent, scale, importance, significance.   The magnitude of the earthquake was such that it caused widespread destruction across the region. حَجْم

magnum opus   a great work, especially the greatest achievement of an artist, writer, or composer.   Masterpiece, great work, crowning achievement, chief work, major work.   Many consider Beethoven's Ninth Symphony to be his magnum opus, a composition that stands as a testament to his genius.   رائِعَة-أعظم ما أبدع

malaprop   the mistaken use of a word in place of a similar-sounding one, often with an unintentionally amusing effect.   Misuse, error, blunder, misstatement, solecism.   Her speech was filled with malaprops, such as saying "dance a flamingo" instead of "dance a flamenco," which made the audience chuckle.   إِسْتِخْدام غَيْر صَحِيح لِلْكَلِمَات

malice   the intention or desire to do evil or cause harm to others.   Spite, malevolence, ill will, malignity, hatred.   The anonymous letter was written with such malice that it left the recipient feeling deeply hurt and threatened.   حِقْد

malignant   something very dangerous or harmful in influence or effect; often used to describe a severe, progressively worsening disease, especially cancer.   Harmful, injurious, virulent, pernicious, malevolent.   The biopsy revealed that the tumor was malignant, necessitating immediate and aggressive treatment.   خَبِيث

malingers   the act of pretending to be ill or injured to avoid duty or work.   Shirks, feigns illness, dodges, loafs, slacks.   He often malingers to get out of doing chores, but his mother is no longer fooled by his fake coughs and complaints.   يَتَظَاهَر بِالمَرَض

mandate   an official order or commission to do something; it can also refer to the authority granted to carry out a policy or course of action. Directive, order, decree, command, authorization.   The newly elected government received a clear mandate from the voters to implement sweeping healthcare reforms.   تَفْوِيض-انتداب

marauding   roaming about in search of plunder or committing acts of violence, often in a group. Pillaging, raiding, looting, plundering, ravaging. The marauding band of thieves left a trail of destruction as they moved from village to village.   يَسْلُب

marquis   a nobleman of hereditary rank in various European peerages and in some of their former colonies, ranking below a duke and above an earl or count.   Nobleman, aristocrat, lord, peer, noble.   The marquis hosted a grand ball at his estate, inviting all the prominent figures of the region.   أَحَدُ النُّبَلاء-مَارْكِيز

marred   damaged or spoiled to a certain extent, making something less perfect, attractive, or enjoyable.   Damaged, spoiled, blemished, impaired, tarnished.   The beauty of the landscape was marred by the construction of the new highway running through it.   تَشَوَّه

masochist   a person who derives pleasure from their own pain and suffering, especially in a sexual context.   Pain lover, sufferer, flagellant, self-punisher, self-tormenter.   His friends couldn't understand why he seemed to enjoy difficult and grueling challenges, jokingly calling him a masochist.   مَازُوخِي

maxims   short, pithy statements expressing a general truth or rule of conduct.   Aphorisms, proverbs, adages, sayings, axioms. One of his favorite maxims was "Actions speak louder than words," which he tried to live by every day. حِكَم

meager   describes something that is deficient in quantity or quality; lacking in richness, fullness, or strength.   Scanty, sparse, insufficient, paltry, inadequate.   The family's meager income made it difficult for them to afford basic necessities. ضَئِيل

meddle   means to interfere in something that is not one's concern, often in a way that is unwelcome or intrusive.   Interfere, intrude, pry, tamper, butt in.   She warned her neighbor not to meddle in her personal affairs, as it was none of his business. يَتَدَخَّل-تَطَفَّل

mementoes   objects kept as reminders or souvenirs of a person, place, or event. Souvenirs, keepsakes, tokens, memorabilia, remembrances.   She kept a box of mementoes from her travels around the world, each item holding special memories. تَذْكَارَات

menagerie   a collection of wild animals kept in captivity for exhibition, or a strange or diverse collection of people or things.   Zoo, collection, exhibition, assemblage, assortment.   The eccentric millionaire's estate featured a menagerie of exotic animals, drawing visitors from far and wide. مَجْمُوعَة حَيَوَانَات-معرض الوحوش

mendacity   untruthfulness or a tendency to lie; it can also mean a falsehood or lie itself.   Deceit, dishonesty, falsehood, lying, untruthfulness.   The politician's mendacity was exposed by the investigative journalist, leading to a loss of public trust.   كَذِب

menial   work that is lowly and sometimes degrading, typically involving domestic tasks and requiring little skill or training.   Lowly, humble, unskilled, servile, degrading.   Despite his college degree, he had to take on menial jobs to make ends meet.   وَضيع

merit   the quality of being particularly good or worthy, especially so as to deserve praise or reward.   Excellence, worth, value, virtue, quality.   Her proposal has considerable merit and should be considered carefully by the committee.   جَدَارَة

mint   1. an aromatic herb known for its fresh and cooling flavor. 2. a place where coins are produced under government authority. 3. to produce or create something, especially coins. 1. Peppermint, spearmint, mentha. 2. Coinage, treasury, minting. 3. Create, produce, forge.   1. She added fresh mint leaves to her iced tea for a refreshing twist. 2. The old mint was converted into a museum showcasing historical currency. 3. The government decided to mint a new series of commemorative coins.   عُشْبَة النَّعْنَاع-دَار السَّكّ-يَسْكّ الذُّقُود

mirth   amusement, especially as expressed in laughter.   Glee, joy, merriment, cheerfulness, hilarity.   The children's mirth filled the room as they played and laughed together. بَهْجَة

mirthless   a lack of genuine amusement or happiness, often appearing as a forced or joyless smile or laugh.   Joyless, gloomy, dismal, cheerless, bleak. His mirthless laugh did nothing to hide the sadness in his eyes.   خَالٍ مِنَ الفَرَح

misbegotten   something that is badly conceived, designed, or planned; it can also mean illegitimate or born out of wedlock.   Ill-conceived, ill-advised, poorly planned, illegitimate, bastard. The company's misbegotten attempt to expand into a new market resulted in significant financial losses.   سَيِّء التَّدْبِير

missive   a written message, especially a long or official letter.   Letter, message, communication, note, epistle.   She received a lengthy missive from her friend, detailing all the events of the past year.   رِسَالَة

moat   a deep, wide ditch, typically filled with water, that surrounds a castle, fortification, or town, intended as a defense against attack.   Ditch, trench, channel, fosse, watercourse.   The ancient castle was protected by a wide moat, making it difficult for invaders to breach its walls.   خَنْدَق

monastic   a way of life dedicated to religious practice and often characterized by seclusion, simplicity, and austerity, typically within a monastery.   Ascetic, cloistered, reclusive, hermitic, contemplative. He chose a monastic lifestyle, living in solitude and dedicating his days to prayer and meditation.   رَهْبَانِي

monolith   a large single upright block of stone, especially one shaped into or serving as a pillar or monument. It can also refer to an organization or structure that is large, powerful, indivisible, and slow to change.   Stone, pillar, column, obelisk, megalith.

The ancient monolith stood in the center of the desert, a testament to the engineering skills of the past civilization.   صَدْرَة عِمْلاقَة-قائم صخرى

morbid   an unhealthy or abnormal interest in disturbing and unpleasant subjects, especially death and disease.   Ghoulish, macabre, gruesome, unhealthy, unwholesome.   His morbid fascination with crime stories often left his friends feeling uncomfortable.   ّمَرَضِي

morgue   a place where dead bodies are kept, typically to be identified or claimed, or for examination and autopsy.   Mortuary, funeral home, depository, repository, chapel of rest.   The detective went to the morgue to identify the body found at the crime scene.   مَشْرَدَة

morose   describes a sullen, gloomy, or ill-tempered mood or disposition.   Sullen, gloomy, glum, moody, despondent.   After hearing the bad news, he became morose and unresponsive, retreating into his room. كَئِيب

morsel   a small piece or amount of food; a bite or mouthful.   Bite, piece, bit, chunk, fragment.   She savored every morsel of the delicious chocolate cake, not wanting it to end.   لُقْمَة

mortifying   causing someone to feel extremely embarrassed, ashamed, or humiliated.   Humiliating, embarrassing, shaming, discomfiting, degrading.   Forgetting her lines in front of the packed

audience was a mortifying experience for the young
actress. مُذِلّ

mosaic   a picture or pattern produced by
arranging together small colored pieces of hard
material, such as stone, tile, or glass.   Collage,
montage, inlay, tessellation, assemblage.   The
church's floor was covered with an intricate mosaic
depicting scenes from the Bible.   فُسَيْفِسَاء

motley   something that is composed of a diverse and
often incongruous mix of elements or colors.   Mixed,
varied, diverse, heterogeneous, assorted.   The
festival attracted a motley crowd of artists, musicians,
and enthusiasts from all over the world.   مُتَنَوِّع

mottled   something that is marked with spots or
smears of color.   Spotted, speckled, blotchy,
dappled, streaked.   The horse's coat was a beautiful
mottled pattern of brown and white. مُرَقَّط

mundane   refers to something that is ordinary,
commonplace, or lacking in excitement; it can also
relate to the earthly, as opposed to the spiritual.
     Ordinary, everyday, routine, banal, prosaic. She
longed for adventure and excitement to break the
monotony of her mundane life.   دُنْيَوِي

mutability   the quality of being changeable or
subject to change.   Changeability, variability, fluidity,
alterability, adaptability.   The mutability of the
weather in the mountains made it difficult to plan
outdoor activities.   قَابِلِيَّة لِلتَّغَيُّر

myrmidon   a loyal follower or subordinate, especially one who executes orders unquestioningly or unscrupulously.   Follower, subordinate, henchman, minion, adherent. The dictator's myrmidons carried out his harsh policies without question, enforcing his rule with an iron fist.   تَابِع مُطيع

necromantic   pertains to necromancy, which is the practice of communicating with the dead, often to predict the future or influence events.   Sorcery, witchcraft, black magic, divination, occultism.   The old legend spoke of a necromantic ritual that could summon spirits from the underworld to answer questions from the living.   سِحْرِيّ مَرْبُوط بِالشَّعْوَذَة

necrophagist   describes a creature that consumes corpses, it can also mean man-eating or consumption of human carcasses.   cannibalistic   the necrophagist criminal used to eat the bodies of his victims.   آكل لحم الجثث

nefarious   actions that are extremely wicked or criminal in nature.   Wicked, evil, villainous, sinful, heinous.   The nefarious plot of the supervillain aimed to destroy the city and all its inhabitants.   شَرَّ- شنيع

neophyte   a person who is new to a subject, skill, or belief; a beginner or novice. Novice, beginner, newcomer, apprentice, fledgling.   As a neophyte in the world of cooking, she eagerly followed recipes to learn new techniques. مُبْتَدِئ

niche   1. a shallow recess, especially one in a wall to display a statue or ornament. 2. a comfortable or suitable position in life or employment. 3. a specialized segment of the market for a particular kind of product or service.   1. Recess, alcove, hollow, cavity. 2.

Position, role, function, specialty. 3. Market segment, sector, category.   1. The statue of the saint was placed in a niche in the cathedral's wall. 2. She found her niche as a freelance graphic designer after years of working in advertising. 3. The company carved out a niche in the market by focusing on sustainable and eco-friendly products.   رُكْن-مَوْضِع-دور-فَراغُ السُّوق

niggardliness   the quality of being excessively stingy or miserly, unwilling to spend or give freely. Stinginess, miserliness, parsimony, tightfistedness, frugality.   His niggardliness prevented him from contributing to the charity, despite his wealth.   بَخِل

nimble   someone or something that is quick and light in movement or action, agile, or able to move quickly and easily.   Agile, quick, spry, lively, swift, svelte The gymnast's nimble movements impressed the judges during her routine.   سَرِيع-رَشِيق

nipped   to pinch, squeeze, or bite sharply, often causing a sudden, sharp pain.   Pinched, squeezed, bitten, gripped.   She yelped when the cold wind nipped at her exposed cheeks. عض

non-chalant   a person who appears calm, relaxed, and unconcerned, often in a situation where others might expect them to be worried or anxious. Casual, indifferent, unconcerned, cool, composed.   He acted nonchalant about the upcoming exam, though secretly he was nervous.   لامُبَالٍ

noncessation   describes something that never stops.   continuous, never stopping, meeting no end, endless.   the noncessation of the babys wails frustrated his parents and annoyed the next door.   لا نهاية-مستمر-ابدي

nonentity   a person or thing with no special or interesting qualities; someone or something that is insignificant or unimportant.   Nobody, nonentity, nonperson, lightweight, cipher.   He was dismissed as a nonentity in the corporate world, despite his years of experience.   عديم الأهمية

nook and cranny   refers to every small or hidden place or corner, especially within a confined space or area.   Corner, crevice, recess, cavity, hiding place.   She searched every nook and cranny of the attic for the old family photographs.   كُلّ زاوية وذَقَطة

normalcy   the condition or state of being normal, usual, or typical, especially after a period of disruption or abnormality.   Normality, routine, regularity, standard state.   After the chaos of the storm, the town gradually returned to a sense of normalcy.   الحالة الطبيعية

nosegays   small bouquets of flowers, typically fragrant ones, carried or worn as a decoration or to ward off unpleasant smells.   Posy, bouquet, bunch, spray, corsage.   She received a beautiful nosegay of roses and lilies on her birthday.   بُقْدُوذَة-أكاليل-باقةُ زهرٍ صغيرة

notarize   to certify or attest a document by a notary public, usually by affixing a signature and seal, confirming the authenticity of the signatures on the document.　　　Authenticate, certify, validate, legalize, witness.　　　She had to notarize the legal documents before they could be submitted to the court. تَوْثِيق

novitiate　　　the period or state of being a novice, especially in a religious order or organization, typically involving a period of probation or training before full membership or acceptance.　　　Novicehood, probation, training period, initiation.　　　During her novitiate, she dedicated herself to learning the rituals and disciplines of the monastery.　　　فترة التدريب في الرهبنة-تَرَهِبُن

nudge　　　to push gently or elbow lightly, especially to attract attention, indicate direction, or encourage someone to act or move.　　　Poke, prod, push, elbow, prompt.　　　She nudged her friend to remind him of their agreed-upon signal.　　　دَفْعَة خَفِيفَة

nuisance　　　something or someone that causes inconvenience, annoyance, or harm, especially repeatedly.　　　Bother, annoyance, inconvenience, irritation, disturbance.　　　The loud music from the neighbors was becoming a nuisance to the entire apartment complex.　　　إزعاج

nunnery　　　a place where nuns live and practice a religious life, typically under vows of poverty, chastity, and obedience.　　　Convent, monastery, abbey, cloister.　　　She entered the nunnery at a young age to devote her life to prayer and service.　　　الدير

nystagmus　　　a condition characterized by involuntary, rapid, and repetitive movements of the eyes. It can manifest as side-to-side, up-and-down, or rotary movements of the eyes, which may affect vision and balance.   The patient's nystagmus made it challenging for them to maintain focus on objects for an extended period.   نَغْزُ المَرَذَـةـرَ أرَأة

O o

obdurate   someone who is stubbornly persistent in wrongdoing, refusing to change their opinions or actions despite persuasion or appeals.   Stubborn, unyielding, inflexible, obstinate, adamant.   Despite numerous warnings, he remained obdurate in his decision to quit his job without notice.   عَنِيد

obituary   a notice of someone's death, often including a brief biography or summary of their life, typically published in a newspaper or online. Death notice, necrology, memorial, tribute.   The family wrote a heartfelt obituary to honor their beloved grandmother's life and legacy.   نَعْي

obscurantism   the practice of deliberately preventing the facts or full details of something from becoming known, often for ideological reasons or to maintain ignorance.   Obscurity, concealment, secrecy, suppression, censorship.   The regime's obscurantism regarding the political protests only fueled public distrust and speculation.   التعتيم-ظَلامية

obsequious   Showing excessive willingness to serve or please others; overly submissive or fawning.   Fawning, servile, sycophantic, subservient, groveling   The new assistant was so obsequious that it made everyone in the office uncomfortable, as he seemed to agree with everything the boss said without question.   مُتَذَلِّل

obstreperous   Noisy and difficult to control; unruly.
Unruly, rowdy, boisterous, disruptive, disorderly
The obstreperous crowd at the concert made it difficult for security to maintain order, as people kept pushing and shouting. مُشَاغِب

obtruding   Imposing oneself or one's ideas on others in an unwelcome or intrusive manner.
Intruding, imposing, interfering, meddling, interrupting   Despite not being invited, he kept obtruding on our conversation, offering unsolicited advice that no one wanted to hear.   مُتَدَخِّل

occult   Relating to mystical, supernatural, or magical powers, practices, or phenomena; hidden or secret.
Mystical, supernatural, esoteric, arcane, hidden
She had a deep interest in the occult, spending hours studying ancient texts and practicing rituals meant to harness supernatural powers.   غَامِض

odious   extremely unpleasant; repulsive.
Revolting, repugnant, abhorrent, loathsome, detestable   His odious behavior at the party made everyone want to leave early, as he insulted guests and acted in a shockingly rude manner.   بَغِيض

officiousness   The quality of being assertive of authority in an annoyingly domineering way, especially with regard to petty or trivial matters; intrusive or meddlesome behavior.   Meddlesomeness, intrusiveness, interference, nosiness, pushiness   Her officiousness at work irritated her colleagues, as she constantly interfered in tasks that were not her responsibility and offered unsolicited advice. تَدَخُّل زَائِد

oligarchy   A form of government in which power is held by a small group of people, typically distinguished by wealth, family, or military control. Plutocracy, junta, ruling class, elite group, authoritarianism   The country was governed by an oligarchy, where only a few wealthy families had control over all political and economic decisions. الأُولِيجَارْكِيَّة

ominously   In a way that suggests that something bad or unpleasant is going to happen; forebodingly. Threateningly, forebodingly, menacingly, portentously, gloomily   The sky darkened ominously as the storm approached, and everyone hurried to find shelter before the heavy rain began. بِشَكْل مُنْذِر بِالسُّوء

omnipotence   The quality of having unlimited or very great power. All-powerfulness, almightiness, supreme power, unlimited power, sovereignty   In many religions, omnipotence is an attribute ascribed to deities, believed to have the power to control everything in the universe. قُدْرَة مُطْلَقَة

omnipotent   Having unlimited power and able to do anything; all-powerful. All-powerful, almighty, supreme, invincible, sovereign   The ancient deity was believed to be omnipotent, capable of creating and destroying worlds with a mere thought. قَادِر عَلَى كُلّ شَيْء-جَبَّار

omnipresent   Present everywhere at the same time; widely or constantly encountered.   Ubiquitous, pervasive, universal, all-present, ever-present   In the digital age, social media has become omnipresent,

influencing nearly every aspect of our daily lives.
حَاضِر في كُلّ مَكَان-كلى الوجود

omniscience   The state of knowing everything; infinite
knowledge.   All-knowingness, infinite knowledge,
supreme wisdom, complete awareness, total
understanding In many religious beliefs, God is
attributed with omniscience, having the ability to know
all things past, present, and future.   مَعْرِفَة شَامِلَة-المَعْرِفة
الكُلِّية

omnivorous   Eating both plant and animal
substances; having a wide-ranging diet.   All-eating,
undiscriminating, varied diet, consuming everything,
generalist   Humans are generally omnivorous,
capable of consuming a diverse diet that includes fruits,
vegetables, meats, and grains.   آكِل لِكُلّ شَيْء

opacity   The quality of being opaque; not
allowing light to pass through; the state of being difficult
to understand or unclear.   Opaqueness, non-
transparency, obscurity, murkiness, ambiguity
The opacity of the company's financial statements made
it difficult for investors to understand the true state of its
finances.   غَمُوض

opaque   Not able to be seen through; not
transparent; difficult to understand or explain.
        Non-transparent, cloudy, obscure, unclear,
murky The frosted glass windows were opaque,
providing privacy while still allowing some light to filter
through.   غَيْر شَفَّاف-مُبهَم

ophthalmic   Relating to the eye and its diseases.
Optical, ocular, visual, eye-related, vision-related
The ophthalmic surgeon performed a delicate
procedure to correct the patient's vision, restoring clarity
and improving quality of life. عَيْنِي

opt   To make a choice or decision from a range of
possibilities.   Choose, select, decide, pick, go for
        Given the various options available for the
project, she decided to opt for the most cost-effective
solution.   يَخْتَار

ores   Naturally occurring solid materials from which a
metal or valuable mineral can be profitably extracted.
        Minerals, deposits, rocks, raw materials, lodes
        The geologists discovered rich ores of copper
and gold in the mountain, sparking a rush of mining
activity in the region. خَامَات

orifice   An opening, particularly one in the body,
through which something can pass. Opening, aperture,
hole, outlet, vent   The surgeon carefully
examined the orifice to ensure there was no obstruction
before proceeding with the operation.   فَتْحَة

oscillate   To move or swing back and forth at a
regular speed; to waver between different opinions or
actions.   Swing, sway, fluctuate, vacillate,
alternate   The pendulum of the old grandfather
clock continued to oscillate steadily, marking the
passage of time with each swing.   يَتَذَبْذَب

ossified   Turned into bone or bony tissue; having
become rigid or fixed in attitude or position. Hardened,

calcified, fossilized, rigid, inflexible   Over time, the once innovative company had ossified, sticking to outdated practices and resisting any form of change.   مُتَحَجِّر

ostensible   Stated or appearing to be true, but not necessarily so.   Apparent, seeming, supposed, alleged, superficial   The ostensible reason for the meeting was to discuss the new project, but it soon became clear that there were other hidden agendas.   ظَاهِرِي

ostentatious   Characterized by vulgar or pretentious display; designed to impress or attract notice.   Showy, pretentious, flamboyant, extravagant, gaudy   His ostentatious display of wealth, with flashy cars and expensive jewelry, made him the center of attention at every party.   مُتَبَاهٍ

ostracism   Exclusion from a society or group; the act of deliberately excluding someone from social or professional circles.   Exclusion, shunning, banishment, isolation, rejection   The ostracism she faced after voicing her controversial opinions made her feel lonely and alienated from her colleagues.   نَبْذ

ostracize   To exclude someone from a society or group; to shun or isolate someone.   Exclude, shun, banish, isolate, reject   The community decided to ostracize the man after he was found guilty of dishonesty and deceit.   يَنْبُذ

overarching   Comprehensive or all-encompassing; dominating or encompassing all other aspects.   All-encompassing, comprehensive, inclusive, overall, encompassing The overarching goal of the organization is to improve the quality of education for all students, regardless of their background. شَامِل

overbearing Unpleasantly or arrogantly domineering.
Domineering, authoritarian, imperious, oppressive, bossy His overbearing manner made it difficult for anyone to enjoy working with him, as he constantly tried to control every aspect of the project. مُتَسَلِّط

overscrupulous Excessively concerned with details or morals; meticulous to an extreme degree.
Meticulous, fastidious, pedantic, overprecise, finicky Her overscrupulous nature meant that every report she submitted was flawless, but it also caused significant delays in meeting deadlines. مُتَدَقِّق بِشَكْل مُفْرِط

P p

painstakingly   With great care and thoroughness.   Meticulously, carefully, diligently, thoroughly, conscientiously   She painstakingly researched every detail of her project, ensuring that her presentation was both accurate and impressive.
بِإِجْتِهَادٍ شَدِيد

palliative   Relieving pain or alleviating a problem without dealing with the underlying cause.   Soothing, alleviating, mitigating, comforting, easing   The doctor prescribed palliative care to help the patient manage her symptoms and improve her quality of life.
تَخْفِيفِي

pallor   An unhealthy pale appearance.   Paleness, pastiness, whiteness, wanes, ashen hue   His sudden pallor alarmed his friends, prompting them to rush him to the nearest hospital.   شُحُوب

palpable   So intense as to seem almost tangible; able to be touched or felt.   Tangible, perceptible, noticeable, detectable, evident   The tension in the room was palpable as everyone awaited the announcement of the winner. مَلْمُوس

pandemonium   Wild and noisy disorder or confusion; uproar.   Chaos, mayhem, bedlam, uproar, tumult When the final whistle blew, pandemonium broke out in the stadium as fans flooded the field to celebrate their team's victory. فَوْضَى عَارِمَة

pandering   Catering to or profiting from the weaknesses or vices of others, often in a way that is considered morally reprehensible.   Catering, indulging, gratifying, satisfying, appeasing   The politician was accused of pandering to the public's fears and prejudices to gain votes, rather than addressing real issues.   إرْضَاء

pantomime   A dramatic entertainment, originating in Roman mime, in which performers express meaning through gestures accompanied by music; or, an absurdly exaggerated piece of behavior.   Mime, gesture, charade, wordless performance, acting   The children's laughter filled the theater as they watched the clown perform an elaborate pantomime, conveying the story without a single word.   تَمْثِيل إِيمَائِي

paragon   A person or thing regarded as a perfect example of a particular quality; a model of excellence.   Model, epitome, ideal, exemplar, standard   She was considered the paragon of professionalism, always conducting herself with the utmost integrity and skill.   مِثَال-آيَة-نَمُوذَج

paramilitary   Relating to a group organized similarly to a military force but not part of the official military. Militia, irregulars, auxiliary force, armed group, non-regular soldiers, guerilla   The government deployed paramilitary forces to maintain order during the civil unrest, as they were trained to handle such situations.   شِبْه عَسْكَرِي

paraphernalia   Miscellaneous articles, especially the equipment needed for a particular activity.   Equipment, gear, apparatus, tools, accessories   The artist's studio was cluttered with all sorts of paraphernalia, from paintbrushes and canvases to sculpting tools and reference books.   أَدَوَات

pariah   A person who is rejected or ostracized by society or a particular group; an outcast.   Outcast, untouchable, exile, reject, leper   After the scandal, he became a pariah in the community, shunned by friends and colleagues alike.   مَنْبُوذ

parochial   Having a limited or narrow outlook or scope; relating to a parish.   Narrow-minded, provincial, insular, limited, restricted His parochial views on international relations prevented him from seeing the broader implications of the policy changes.   ضَيِّقُ الأُفُق

parochialism   A narrow, limited, or provincial perspective; a focus on local concerns to the exclusion of wider contexts.   Narrow-mindedness, insularity, provincialism, localism, small-mindedness   The company's parochialism hindered its ability to compete globally, as it failed to consider the broader market trends and international demands.   ضِيقُ أُفُق-مَحْدُودية التفكير

paroxysm   A sudden and violent expression of a particular emotion or activity; a sudden attack or outburst of a disease or symptom.   Outburst, spasm, fit, eruption, convulsion   He was seized by a paroxysm of coughing that left him gasping for breath.   ذَوْبَة

parse To analyze a sentence into its parts and describe their syntactic roles; to examine or analyze minutely. Analyze, dissect, deconstruct, break down, examine The linguist was able to parse the complex sentence, breaking it down into its grammatical components for the students. يُحَلِّل

parsimony Extreme unwillingness to spend money or use resources; stinginess. Stinginess, frugality, miserliness, thriftiness, penny-pinching His parsimony was evident when he refused to contribute to the office gift, despite having a well-paying job. بُخْل

passable Just good enough to be acceptable; satisfactory but not outstanding. Adequate, satisfactory, acceptable, decent, fair The restaurant's food was passable, but it wasn't good enough to make me want to return. مَقْبُول

pathbreaking Being innovative and pioneering; introducing new ideas or methods. Innovative, pioneering, groundbreaking, trailblazing, revolutionary The scientist's pathbreaking research opened up new possibilities for treatment and prevention of the disease. رَائِد-مبتكر

pathos a quality that evokes pity or sadness; an appeal to emotion in literature or speech. Emotion, poignancy, sentimentality, poignance, sadness The pathos in the movie was so powerful that it brought the entire audience to tears. الشَّجَن-رثاء-تَحَذُّن

patronym A name derived from the name of a father or paternal ancestor, typically by the addition of a prefix or suffix.Surname, family name, last name, ancestral name, lineage name   In many cultures, a child's surname is a patronym, reflecting the father's name and heritage. اسْم الأَب

patronymic   A name derived from the name of a father or ancestor, typically by the addition of a prefix or suffix. Surname, family name, ancestral name, lineage name, patronym   In Russian culture, the patronymic is an important part of a person's full name, indicating their father's first name. اسْم الأَب

patroon   A landowner in the Dutch colonies in America, especially New York and New Jersey, who had certain privileges and rights under the former Dutch governments. Landowner, proprietor, feudal lord, estate owner, landlord   The patroon held vast tracts of land and had significant influence over the settlers who lived and worked on his estate.   إقْطَاعِي

pawnbroker   A person who lends money at interest on the security of an article pawned.   Pawnshop owner, moneylender, lender, broker, loan shark   Desperate for cash, she took her grandmother's necklace to the pawnbroker and received a loan against its value.   مُرْتَهِن

pedagogical Relating to teaching or education.   Educational, instructional, didactic, teaching, scholastic   The teacher employed various pedagogical techniques to engage her students and enhance their learning experience. تَرْبَوِي

pedagogue   A teacher, especially one who is strict or pedantic.   Teacher, instructor, educator, schoolteacher, tutor   The old pedagogue was known for his strict discipline and high expectations, which pushed his students to excel. مُرَبٍّ-مُعَلِّم

pedantic   Overly concerned with minor details or formalisms, especially in teaching; tending to show off one's learning. Meticulous, precise, scrupulous, fussy, bookish   His pedantic approach to grammar made his writing classes thorough, but some students found the excessive focus on minor rules tedious. مُتَحَذْلِق- مُتَفَلْسِف

pedigree   The recorded ancestry or lineage of a person or animal; a background or history of a person or thing, especially as it relates to excellence or distinction.   Ancestry, lineage, heritage, descent, genealogy   The breeder proudly displayed the champion dog's pedigree, showcasing its impressive lineage of award-winning ancestors. نَسَب

peerless   Unequaled; unrivaled; having no equal.   Unmatched, incomparable, unparalleled, unrivaled, supreme   Her talent on the violin was peerless, captivating audiences around the world with performances that no one else could match. لا نَظير لَه

pejorative   Expressing contempt or disapproval; having a disparaging, derogatory, or belittling effect.   Disparaging, derogatory, belittling, demeaning, insulting   The article was criticized for its pejorative language, which unfairly portrayed the community in a negative light. ازْدِرائِيّ-احْتِقَارِي

penal servitude   A term of imprisonment during which the prisoner is required to perform hard labor.   Hard labor, imprisonment with labor, forced labor, penal labor, incarceration with hard labor   The judge sentenced the convicted felon to ten years of penal servitude for his crimes, requiring him to work on state projects during his imprisonment.   عُقُوبَة سِجْن مَعَ الأَعْمَال الشَّاقَّة

penchant   A strong or habitual liking for something or a tendency to do something.   Liking, preference, inclination, tendency, fondness   She has a penchant for collecting rare books, and her library is filled with unique and valuable editions.   مَيْل

penitence   The feeling of regret or remorse for having done something wrong; repentance. Remorse, contrition, repentance, regret, guilt   In a sincere display of penitence, he apologized to everyone he had wronged and sought to make amends for his actions.   نَدَم

pensive   Engaged in, involving, or reflecting deep or serious thought.   Thoughtful, reflective, contemplative, meditative, introspective   She sat by the window in a pensive mood, lost in thoughts about her future and the choices she had to make. مُتَأَمِّل

pensiveness   The state of being deeply or seriously thoughtful, often with a tinge of sadness.   Thoughtfulness, reflectiveness, contemplation, introspection, melancholy   His pensiveness was evident as he stared out the window, clearly lost in serious and profound thoughts about life. تَأَمُّل

perambulation   The act of walking around a place, especially for pleasure and in a leisurely way.   Stroll, walk, promenade, ramble, saunter During their perambulation through the old town, they discovered charming cafes and hidden gardens. تَجَوُّل

perceptibly   In a way that can be seen or noticed; noticeably.   Noticeably, visibly, detectably, discernibly, evidently The temperature dropped perceptibly as the sun set, and everyone began to shiver. بِشَكْل مَلْمُوس

perdition   A state of eternal punishment and damnation into which a sinful and unrepentant person passes after death.   Damnation, hell, ruin, doom, destruction   The preacher warned the congregation about the dangers of sin and the inevitability of perdition for those who do not repent. هَلاك

peregrination   A journey, especially a long or meandering one.   Journey, voyage, excursion, pilgrimage, expedition, escapade   After years of peregrination, she finally found her way back home. ارتحال-رحلة طويلة

perfidious   Deceitful and untrustworthy; treacherous.   Treacherous, deceitful, faithless, dishonest, untrustworthy. The perfidious actions of the spy jeopardized the entire mission.   خَائِن-غَادِر

perforate   To pierce or make a hole or holes in something.   Pierce, puncture, penetrate, perforate.   The machine was designed to efficiently perforate sheets of paper.   فتّاح-ثَقَب-ثَغَر

peril   Serious and immediate danger.   Danger, risk, hazard, jeopardy.   They ventured into the jungle despite the obvious peril.   خَطَر

perilous   Full of danger or risk. Dangerous, hazardous, risky, unsafe.   The mountain climbers faced a perilous journey up the icy slope.   خَطِر

permeates   To spread throughout something; to pervade.   Pervade, penetrate, infiltrate, saturate.   The scent of freshly baked bread permeates the kitchen.   يتخلل

pernicious   Having a harmful effect, especially in a gradual or subtle way.Harmful, damaging, destructive, detrimental.   The pernicious influence of gossip can destroy trust among friends.   ضارّ

perpendicular   Intersecting at or forming a right angle (90 degrees).   Vertical, upright, orthogonal, at right angles.   The flagpole stood perpendicular to the ground.   مُتعامِد

pertinent   Relevant or applicable to a particular matter; appropriate.   Relevant, applicable, related, germane.   Her comments were always pertinent to the discussion at hand.   ذو صِلة

perturbation Disturbance or agitation, especially of a public kind.   Disturbance, turmoil, unrest, agitation.   The political scandal caused significant perturbation among the population. اضطراب

perusal   The action of reading or examining something carefully. Examination, scrutiny, study, inspection.   After a quick perusal of the document, she identified several errors. فحص-تمعّن-مُطَالَعَة

peruse   To read or examine something carefully and thoroughly.   Study, scrutinize, inspect, examine.   He perused the contract before signing it. تصفّح-طَالَع-قَلّب

pervade   To spread throughout and be perceived in every part of something.   Permeate, penetrate, suffuse, fill.   The scent of jasmine pervaded the entire garden. انتشر

perverse   Showing a deliberate and obstinate desire to behave in a way that is unreasonable or unacceptable, often in spite of the consequences. Contrary, obstinate, wayward, stubborn.   His perverse sense of humor always seemed to get him into trouble. مُعَكِّر

perversion   The alteration of something from its original course, meaning, or state to a distortion or corruption of what was first intended. Distortion, corruption, deviation, misrepresentation.   The novel explores themes of moral perversion and decay. الإنحراف-إفساد

pesky   Something annoyingly persistent or troublesome.   Annoying, bothersome, irritating, troublesome.   The pesky mosquito kept buzzing around despite our efforts to swat it away.   مُزعِج

pettifogging   Placing undue emphasis on petty details; quibbling over trivial matters. Nitpicking, quibbling, petty, insignificant. The lawyers engaged in pettifogging arguments that delayed the trial unnecessarily. مُدَقَّيِّن-مشتغل بالتوافه

pettily   In a small-minded or mean way; with undue concern for trivial matters.   Small-mindedly, meanly, narrowly, insignificantly.   He responded pettily to her criticism, focusing on minor details rather than the main issue.   بِغَرابَة

petulance   The quality of being childishly sulky or bad-tempered.Irritability, peevishness, sulkiness, crankiness.   His petulance showed when he didn't get his way during the meeting.   سُخط-نَكَد

petulant   Childishly sulky or bad-tempered.   Irritable, peevish, moody, testy.   The child became petulant when she was denied a second piece of cake.   رديء الخلق

pews   Long benches with backs, used for seating in churches or other places of worship. Church seating   The church was filled with parishioners sitting in wooden pews. دَوْرَق-مقاعد

phallic   Relating to or resembling a penis, especially in shape. Penis-shaped, phallus-like, suggestive of a penis.   The ancient sculpture had a distinctly phallic appearance.   قضيبيّ

phantasmagoria   A sequence of real or imaginary images, like those seen in a dream. Fantasy, illusion, hallucination, dream. The artist's paintings created a phantasmagoria of colors and shapes.   تخيُّلات-أوهام

philandering   Engaging in casual or frequent love affairs, especially when married.   Womanizing, flirting, cheating, infidelity.   His reputation as a philandering playboy preceded him wherever he went.   يغَازل-مُداعَبَة

philanthropy   The desire to promote the welfare of others, usually through charitable donations or actions.   Charity, humanitarianism, benevolence, generosity.   His philanthropy extended to funding education programs in underprivileged communities.   إنسَانذرِيّة-إِحسان

philippic   A bitter verbal attack or denunciation, especially a lengthy one.   Tirade, diatribe, harangue, rant.   The politician delivered a fiery philippic against his opponents during the debate.   سلسلة شتائم-كلمة حادة-هجوم لفظي

philistine   A materialistic person who is hostile or indifferent to culture and the arts, or who has no understanding or appreciation of them.   Uncultured, uncivilized, boorish, ignorant. He was often dismissed as a philistine because of his disdain for classical literature.   مادّيّ-عدواني للفكر-كاره للأدب والثقافة

phlegmatic   Having an unemotional and calm disposition, especially in situations of stress or excitement.   Calm, composed, impassive, stoic.   Her phlegmatic demeanor helped her remain calm during the crisis.   بارد-بَلْغَمِيُّ المَزاج

piecemeal   Done or made in a gradual way, one piece at a time, or in a disconnected or fragmentary manner.   Gradual, bit by bit, in stages, disjointed.   They renovated the old house piecemeal, starting with the roof and working their way down.   تَدريجي-شَيْئاً فَشَيْئا

pilloried   To publicly criticize or ridicule someone harshly or severely.   Criticized, denounced, condemned, censured.   The politician was pilloried in the press for his controversial remarks.   هُتِمَ شُ-سخر

piqued   To stimulate interest or curiosity, especially in a slight degree.   Stimulated, aroused, provoked, intrigued.   Her curiosity was piqued by the mysterious letter left on her doorstep.   أثار

pivot   To turn or rotate, especially on a central point; to change direction or course.   Rotate, turn, revolve, shift.   The company decided to pivot its business strategy towards online sales.   دَوْرَان

pivotal   Of crucial importance; central to something.   Crucial, critical, essential, key.   His pivotal role in the negotiation process ensured the success of the deal.   حاسِم-أَسَاسِيّ-جَوهَرِي

placable   Capable of being appeased or pacified; inclined to forgive or overlook offenses.   Forgiving, lenient, tolerant, gentle.   Despite his anger, he was eventually placable and willing to reconcile. قابِل لِلتَّسامُح- صَفُوح

plebeian   Of or characteristic of the common people; lacking refinement or sophistication. Common, ordinary, vulgar, lowborn.   The artist preferred to depict plebeian life rather than aristocratic scenes. شَعْبِي

plebeianism   The quality or state of being plebeian; characteristic of or pertaining to the common people.   Commonness, vulgarity, ordinariness.   The author criticized the novel for its plebeianism, arguing it lacked depth and sophistication.   الشعبوية

plenipotentiary   A person, especially a diplomat, invested with full power to act on behalf of their government.   Ambassador, envoy, representative, delegate.   The plenipotentiary was authorized to negotiate and sign the peace treaty on behalf of the country.   مُفَوَّض

plethora   An excessive amount or abundance of something.   Excess, surplus, abundance, profusion.   The store offered a plethora of options for shoppers to choose from.   كثرة-زِيَادَة

ploughed   1. To turn up soil using a plough (plow), typically for planting crops. 2. To fail or be unsuccessful, especially in an exam or academic endeavor.   1. Tilled, cultivated, furrowed. 2. Failed, bombed, flunked.

1. The farmer ploughed the field in preparation for planting wheat. 2. Despite studying hard, he ploughed his chemistry exam. محروث-حرث-فشل

plunder To steal goods from (a place or person), typically using force and in a time of war or civil disorder. Loot, pillage, ransack, sack. The invaders plundered the village, taking everything of value. نَهَب

plurality The state of being plural, or the fact of consisting of many different elements. Diversity, multiplicity, variety, assortment. The city prided itself on its cultural plurality, celebrating various traditions and beliefs. التعدد

pogrom An organized massacre or persecution of a particular ethnic group, especially Jews. Massacre, persecution, slaughter, massacre. The pogrom in the city led to the displacement of thousands of innocent civilians. المذبحة المدبرة

poignancy The quality of evoking a keen sense of sadness or regret; deeply moving. Emotion, feeling, pathos, sadness. The poignancy of the film's ending left everyone in tears. شدّة الحزن-المرارة

polling booth A place where voters go to cast their votes in an election. voting room. Citizens lined up outside the polling booth to exercise their democratic right. غُرْفَةُ التَّصْوِيت

polysemy The coexistence of many possible meanings for a word or phrase. Ambiguity, multiple meanings, versatility, multivocality, equivocacy.   The polysemy of "light" includes illumination, not heavy, and understanding.   تَعَدُّدُ المَعَاني

pomposity   The quality of being pompous; self-importance or excessive dignity.   Arrogance, haughtiness, self-importance, pretentiousness.
His pomposity during the meeting irritated everyone present.   التكبر

pontificate   To speak or express opinions in a pompous or dogmatic way.   Lecture, sermonize, preach, declaim.   He loved to pontificate about politics, often dominating conversations with his strong opinions.   التَبَجُّح

poplar   A type of tall, fast-growing tree with triangular leaves that tremble in the breeze.   The poplar trees lined the riverbank, providing shade and beauty.   الحور

populace   The general public; the common people of a country or region. Population, citizenry, community, public. The new policy sparked concern among the populace about its potential impact on the environment.   الجماهير

portmanteau   A large suitcase or a word blending the sounds and combining the meanings of two others, like brunch, meaning breakfast and lunch.   Blend, compound word, suitcase.   The word smog is a portmanteau of smoke and fog.   حَقِيبَةُ سَفَر-لفظة اقترانية

posit To assume as a fact or take as a given; to put forward as an argument or postulate. Assume, postulate, assert, propose. The theory posits that social interactions shape individual behavior. يُفَرِّض-اِقترح

postmortem 1. An examination or analysis of a situation or event after it has occurred, especially a detailed examination of a deceased body to determine the cause of death. 2. occurring or performed after death. Analysis, review, autopsy, examination, after death. The team conducted a postmortem of the project to identify areas for improvement.
تَشْريح-ما بعد الموت

postpartum Relating to the period immediately after childbirth. After childbirth, postnatal. The new mother experienced postpartum depression after giving birth. ما بَعْدُ الْوُلادَة

postulation The act of putting forward a theory, idea, or argument, especially in a formal or systematic manner. Hypothesis, theory, conjecture, assumption. His postulation about the origins of the universe sparked a lively debate among scientists.
فَرْضية

pout To push out one's lips, especially in annoyance or in a sullen manner. Frown, sulk, grimace, mope. She tends to pout when she doesn't get her way. عَبَسَ

practicable Capable of being done, used, or put into practice successfully; feasible. Feasible, achievable, possible, viable. The plan seemed practicable given the resources and time available. قابِل لِلتَّطْبِيق

prairie   An extensive area of flat or rolling grassland, typically without many trees. plain, grassland, meadow, steppe.   The prairie stretched out for miles, dotted with wildflowers and grazing buffalo. السهول

precepts   Rules or principles intended to regulate behavior or thought; a general rule intended to regulate behavior or thought.   Principles, rules, guidelines, doctrines.   The teacher imparted important life precepts to his students.   مبادئ-تَعَالِيم

precipice   A very steep rock face or cliff, typically a tall one.   Cliff, crag, bluff, brink.   They stood at the edge of the precipice, gazing down into the abyss below. هاوية

precipitate   To cause something to happen suddenly, unexpectedly, or prematurely; to bring about abruptly.   Hasten, accelerate, provoke, trigger.   His reckless actions precipitated a crisis within the company.   يُسَرِّع

prepubescent   Relating to or occurring in the period before puberty.Pre-adolescent, juvenile, immature.   She wrote a book aimed at prepubescent children, addressing their specific developmental needs.قَبْل البُلُوغ

precocity   The quality or state of being unusually advanced or mature in development, especially mental development, for one's age. Early development, giftedness, talent.   Her precocity in music allowed her to perform at a professional level by the age of ten. النضوج المبكر-بُكُور

precursor   A person or thing that comes before another of the same kind; a forerunner or predecessor.   Forerunner, predecessor, harbinger, antecedent.   The invention of the steam engine was a precursor to the Industrial Revolution.   سابِق-سَلَف

predilection   A preference or special liking for something; a bias in favor of something.   Preference, inclination, liking, penchant.   She had a predilection for spicy food, often choosing dishes with extra chili peppers.   ميلاً-انحِياز

preening   1. To groom oneself, especially by licking the fur or feathers with the beak or tongue, as birds do. 2. devote effort to making oneself look attractive and then admire one's appearance.   Grooming, cleaning, primping, tidying, pride oneself.   1. The cat spent hours preening itself after coming in from the rain. 2. adolescents preening in their bedroom mirrors.   تَزَيِّين-يتبَاهى-يِتَهَنْدَم

prefect   A person appointed to a position of command or authority, especially in certain countries or organizations. monitor, preposter.   The school prefects were responsible for maintaining discipline among the students.   النائِب-النائِب

prejudicial   Harmful or detrimental; causing or likely to cause harm.   Damaging, detrimental, harmful,

adverse. The judge ruled that the evidence was prejudicial to the defendant's case. مضر

preliminary Something that comes before the main part; introductory or preparatory. Initial, preparatory, introductory, provisional. They conducted preliminary research before starting the main experiment. أولي

premeditation The act of thinking about and planning a crime or harmful act beforehand. Planning, deliberation, calculation, foresight,forethought. The prosecutor argued that the crime was committed with premeditation and malice. التررصُّد

premonition A strong feeling or belief that something is going to happen, typically something unpleasant or foreboding, before it occurs. Forewarning, presentiment, intuition, hunch. She had a premonition that something bad was going to happen on the trip. عِلامةٌ سَلَفْيِةٌ-هاجِس

propaedeutic Pertaining to or serving as a preparation or introduction to learning or study. Preliminary, introductory, preparatory. The propaedeutic course provided students with foundational knowledge before they entered more advanced studies. تمهيدي-تدريبي-اولي

prepense Planned or arranged in advance; premeditated. Premeditated, deliberate, intentional, calculated. The prosecutor argued that the crime was committed with malice prepense. بتفكير

preponderance   the quality or fact of being greater in number, quantity, or importance.   Majority, Dominance, Superiority, Prevalence, Predominance   The preponderance of evidence presented in the trial clearly indicated the defendant's guilt.   غَلَبَة-أَكثرية-أَرجَحِيَّة

preposterous refers to something that is utterly absurd or ridiculous, going against common sense or reason.   Absurd, Ridiculous, Ludicrous, Outrageous, Nonsensical   The idea that the Earth is flat is preposterous in light of all the scientific evidence.   سَخِيف

prerogative   a right or privilege exclusive to a particular individual or class. Privilege, Right, Entitlement, Perquisite, Advantage   As the company's founder, she believed it was her prerogative to make the final decision on major issues.   حَقّ-اِمتِياز

pristine   something that is in its original condition, unspoiled, and clean. Unspoiled, Immaculate, Untouched, Clean, Pure   The lake's pristine waters were so clear that you could see the fish swimming at the bottom.   بِكْر-أصلي-ّصاف

pretense   an attempt to make something that is not the case appear true; a false display of feelings, attitudes, or intentions.   Deception, Pretending, Simulation, Sham, Facade   She dropped the pretense of being happy and admitted she was feeling quite sad.   تَظَاهُر-اِدِّعَاء

prevaricate   speaking or acting in an evasive way, often to avoid telling the truth or to mislead. Evade, Dodge, Equivocate, Lie, Mislead   When asked about his whereabouts on the night of the crime, he began to prevaricate, giving vague and confusing answers.
يُرَاوِغ

privation   a state in which essential things such as food and warmth are lacking; the absence of necessities.   Deprivation, Hardship, Poverty, Lack, Destitution   The war left many families in a state of privation, struggling to find enough food and shelter.
حِرِرْمَان-اِفتِقار

privy   1. being aware of or sharing in the knowledge of something private or secret. 2. Hidden or secret.
      Informed, Aware, Cognizant, Acquainted, In the know, secret. 1. As a trusted advisor, she was privy to the company's confidential plans for expansion. 2. He was in his own privy when he had the idea of the business.   مُطَّلِع-خصوصيّ-ذاتِي

Probed   investigating or exploring something thoroughly, especially by using a tool or instrument.
      Investigated, Examined, Explored, Scrutinized, Inspected   The scientist probed the depths of the ocean to discover new forms of marine life. تَدَرَّى-تقصّى

procurator   an official with the power to act on behalf of someone else, especially in legal or administrative matters.   Agent, Administrator, Representative, Steward, Attorney   The procurator was responsible for managing the estate and handling all legal affairs on behalf of the absent owner. مُدِير أَعْمَال-مُفَوّض

prod   poking someone with a finger, foot, or pointed object; it can also mean to stimulate or persuade someone to take action.   Poke, Jab, Nudge, Spur, Urge   She had to prod him several times before he finally got up from the couch to help with the chores.
يَدُثَّ-حَضَض

prodigal   spending money or resources freely and recklessly; wastefully extravagant. It can also describe someone who is lavishly abundant or generous.
    Wasteful, Extravagant, Lavish, Spendthrift, Profligate   The prodigal son returned home after years of reckless spending and irresponsible living.
مُبَذِّر

prodigality   the quality of being wastefully extravagant; lavishness in spending. Extravagance, Wastefulness, Lavishness, Profligacy, Excess   His prodigality led to the rapid depletion of his inheritance, leaving him in financial ruin. تَبْذِير

profanation   the act of treating something sacred with disrespect or irreverence.   Desecration, Defilement, Violation, Irreverence, Sacrilege   The vandalism of the ancient temple was seen as a profanation of a sacred place by the local community. تَدْنِيس

profane   showing disrespect or contempt for sacred things, or to treat something sacred with irreverence.   Irreverent, Blasphemous, Sacrilegious, Impious, Ungodly   His profane language during the ceremony shocked everyone in attendance. مُدَنَّس

profess declaring or claiming something openly or with strong affirmation, often about one's feelings, beliefs, or faith. Declare, Announce, Claim, Affirm, Proclaim She professed her love for him in front of the entire congregation, leaving everyone in awe. يُعْلِن

profundity great depth of insight or knowledge, intellectual or emotional depth, or something that is very deep. Depth, Insight, Wisdom, Intensity, Thoughtfulness The profundity of her speech left the audience in deep reflection about the meaning of life. عُمْق

profusely doing something in a large amount or to a great degree; excessively. Abundantly, Excessively, Lavishly, Generously, Copiously He apologized profusely for his mistake, hoping to make amends with everyone affected. بِغَزَارَة

progeny the descendants or offspring of a person, animal, or plant. Offspring, Descendants, Children, Heirs, Issue The scientist was proud of his academic progeny, seeing his students carry forward his legacy of research. نَسْل

prognosis the likely course or outcome of a disease or condition; a forecast or prediction about how a situation will develop. Forecast, Prediction, Outlook, Projection, Expectation The doctor gave a positive prognosis, indicating that with treatment, the patient should make a full recovery. تَوَقُّع-تكهُّن

prognosticated   having predicted or foretold a future event, typically based on current signs or indications.   Predicted, Forecasted, Foretold, Anticipated, Foreseen The economist prognosticated a recession, warning that various economic indicators pointed to a downturn.   تَذَبَّأَ

prognostication   the action of foretelling or predicting future events based on current signs or indications.   Prediction, Forecast, Prophecy, Anticipation, Foretelling   The scientist's prognostication about the climate changes proved to be alarmingly accurate.   تَذَبُّؤ

projectiles   objects that are thrown, fired, or otherwise propelled, especially as a weapon, such as a bullet or a missile.   Missiles, Bullets, Shells, Arrows, Darts   The ancient warriors used bows and arrows as their primary projectiles during battle.
قَذَائِف

proleptical   anticipating and answering objections before they are raised, or the representation of a future act or development as if it already exists or has already occurred.   Anticipatory, Preemptive, Presumptive, Premature, Forerunning   Her proleptical remarks during the presentation addressed potential concerns before the audience had a chance to voice them.
اِسْتِبَاقِي

proles   an informal term that refers to the working class or lower class of a society, often used in a pejorative or dismissive way. Working class, Commoners, Laborers, Proletariat, Masses In the

dystopian novel, the government kept the proles
uneducated to maintain control over them.   العَامَّةَ-الطبقة
العاملة

proliferation   the rapid increase or spread of
something, especially the rapid multiplication of parts,
cells, or organisms.   Multiplication, Spread,
Expansion, Growth, Escalation   The proliferation of
technology in the past decade has drastically changed
the way we communicate.   اِنْتِشَار

promptitude   the quality of acting quickly and without
delay; punctuality or readiness.   Punctuality,
Promptness, Readiness, Alacrity, Expediency
Her promptitude in responding to the emergency call
saved many lives.   سُرْعَة-عَجَلَة-يقظة

propagate   the action of spreading and promoting
ideas, information, or organisms, particularly in the
context of reproduction or dissemination.   Spread,
Disseminate, Broadcast, Transmit, Multiply The
scientists worked to propagate the endangered plant
species to prevent it from becoming extinct. يَنْشُر

propel   to drive, push, or move something forward or
in a particular direction, often with force.   Drive,
Push, Thrust, Launch, Hurl   The strong wind helped to
propel the sailboat swiftly across the lake.   يَدْفَع

propitiation   the act of appeasing a god, spirit, or
person, often through a sacrifice or offering, to gain
favor or forgiveness. Atonement, Conciliation,
Pacification, Appeasement, Amends The villagers

offered sacrifices as an act of propitiation to ensure a bountiful harvest.   تَكْفِير-اِسْتِرضاء

propitiate   to win or regain the favor of a god, spirit, or person by doing something that pleases them. Appease, Pacify, Conciliate, Mollify, Placate   They built a shrine to propitiate the gods and seek protection for their village.   يُكَفّر-يَسْتَرضي

proprietor   the owner of a business, or a holder of property.   Owner, Possessor, Holder, Landlord, Proprietress for a female proprietor. The proprietor of the small bakery was known for her delicious homemade pastries and friendly service.   مَالِك

proprietorship   the state or condition of being a proprietor, particularly the ownership and management of a business.   Ownership, Possession, Management, Control, Tenure   Her proprietorship of the local bookstore has allowed her to create a cozy and inviting space for book lovers in the community.   مِلْكِيَّة

proprioception   the body's ability to sense its position, motion, and equilibrium. It involves the perception of the relative position of one's own body parts and the strength of effort being employed in movement.   Kinesthetic sense, Body awareness, Position sense, Spatial awareness, Self-perception Athletes often have highly developed proprioception, which helps them move efficiently and avoid injuries.   الإِدْرَاكُ الحِسِّيُّ العَمِيق

prosaic   refers to having the style or diction of prose; lacking poetic beauty. It can also mean ordinary, dull, or unimaginative. Ordinary, Dull, Mundane, Unimaginative, Banal Despite the prosaic nature of his job, he found joy in the small tasks and daily routines. عَادِي-ذَثْرِي

protuberance   something that sticks out from a surface, usually in a rounded or irregular shape.
      Bulge, Protuberance, Bump, Swelling, Projection
      The protuberance on the tree trunk looked like a large, knobby knot.   بُرُوز-اِنْتِفاخ

protruded   to extend beyond or above a surface.
      Jutted, Stuck out, Extended, Projected, Bulged
      A sharp rock protruded from the cliff, making the climb more dangerous.   بَارِز

provision   the action of providing or supplying something for use, or an amount or thing supplied or provided. It can also refer to a condition or requirement in a legal document.   Supply, Providing, Stipulation, Clause, Preparation   The contract included a provision that allowed for annual reviews of performance. تَزْوِيد-تَموِين-مَوَّن

provisional   something arranged or existing for the present, possibly to be changed later; temporary.
      Temporary, Interim, Conditional, Tentative, Transitional   The committee appointed a provisional leader until a permanent one could be elected. مُؤَقَّت

prowling   moving around restlessly and stealthily, especially in search of prey or something to steal.
      Sneaking, Roaming, Lurking, Stalking, Scouting

The cat was prowling through the garden, searching for any unsuspecting birds. يَتَجَوَّلُ- التّطواف خلسة

Proxies   individuals or entities authorized to act on behalf of others, particularly in voting or decision-making contexts. It can also mean a figure that can be used to represent the value of something in a calculation.   Representatives, Agents, Delegates, Surrogates, Substitutes   Shareholders can appoint proxies to vote on their behalf at the annual meeting. وُكَلَاء

prudence   the quality of being cautious, wise, and judicious in practical affairs; exercising good judgment and foresight.   Caution, Wisdom, Judiciousness, Discretion, Sagacity   Her prudence in financial matters helped her save enough money for a comfortable retirement. تَعَقّل-اِحتِراز

prudent   acting with or showing care and thought for the future; exercising good judgment and caution.   Wise, Cautious, Judicious, Sensible, Discreet   It is prudent to save a portion of your income for unexpected expenses. دَكِيم-دَصِديف

prune   trimming or cutting away dead or overgrown branches or stems, especially to encourage growth. It can also mean to reduce or remove unnecessary parts.   Trim, Cut back, Clip, Thin, Pare   It's important to prune the rose bushes in early spring to promote healthy growth and abundant blooms. يُقَلِّم

pry   to inquire too closely into a person's private affairs, often in an intrusive or overly curious manner. It can also refer to using leverage to force something open. Snoop, Intrude, Investigate, Meddle, Probe It's rude to pry into someone's personal life without their permission. يَتَطَفَّل

pugilistic   related to boxing or fighting with the fists; often describing someone who is aggressive or ready to fight.   Combative, Aggressive, Belligerent, Pugnacious, Hostile   His pugilistic nature often got him into trouble, as he was always ready to argue and fight. قِتَالِيّ-تلاكُمي

pulmonary hemorrhage   bleeding from the lungs or airways, which can lead to coughing up blood and respiratory distress.   Lung bleeding, Pulmonary bleeding, Hemoptysis when referring to coughing up blood. The patient was rushed to the emergency room after experiencing severe pulmonary hemorrhage. نَزِيف رِئَوِي

pulpit   a raised platform or lectern in a church or chapel from which the preacher delivers a sermon.   Lectern, Podium, Rostrum, Dais, Platform The minister stepped up to the pulpit to deliver his Sunday sermon to the congregation. مِنْبَر

pulverize   to crush or grind something into a fine powder or dust, typically using mechanical force. Crush, Grind, Smash, Mill, Powder   The old stone mill was used to pulverize grains into flour for baking. يَطْحَن-يَسْحق

puncture   a small hole or wound made by a sharp object, typically resulting in the piercing or penetration of a surface or material.   Hole, Piercing, Perforation, Prick, Poking   She had to go to the hospital to get stitches for a deep puncture wound on her arm.   ثَقْب

punitive   something relating to, or intended as punishment or disciplinary action.   Penal, Retributive, Corrective, Disciplinary, Vindictive   The company implemented punitive measures against employees who violated company policies.   عِقَابِي

puny   something or someone small, weak, or insignificant in size, strength, or importance. Small, Weak, Feeble, Insignificant, Meager   Despite his puny appearance, the young boy displayed remarkable courage in facing his fears.   ضَئِيل-هَزِيل

purgatorial   characteristic of purgatory, a place or state of suffering or purification where souls are believed to be cleansed of sins.   Cleansing, Purifying, Atoning, Penitential   The novel depicted a journey through a purgatorial landscape, where characters faced their past actions and sought redemption.   مُطَهَّر

puritanism   a strict moral or religious movement, particularly in the 16th and 17th centuries, characterized by moral rigor, austerity, and opposition to luxury and indulgence.   Moral rigor, Asceticism, Strictness, Rigidity, Piousness   Puritanism influenced many aspects of early American culture, including laws and social norms.   تَزَمُّت-تَطَهُّرية

purloin   to steal something, especially in a deceitful or secretive way.   Steal, Pilfer, Swipe, Filch, Embezzle   She was caught trying to purloin money from the company's petty cash fund. يَسْرِق

purser   an officer on a ship or aircraft responsible for handling money, passenger accounts, and other financial matters during a voyage.   Steward, Treasurer, Financial officer   The purser on the cruise ship ensured that all financial transactions and accounts were meticulously managed throughout the journey.
خَزَّان-ضابط إداري-امين حسابات

purveyor   a person or entity that supplies or provides goods, services, or provisions, often in a specific trade or industry.   Supplier, Vendor, Provider, Dealer, Supplier   He was known as a purveyor of fine wines and gourmet foods in the local community.   مُزَوِّد-مُوَرِّد

putrid   something that is decaying or rotting, typically emitting a foul smell due to decomposition. Rotten, Decomposed, Spoiled, Rancid, Fetid The garbage left unattended in the heat became putrid and attracted swarms of flies.   فاسِد-مُتَعَفِّن

 Q q

quagmire   a soft, boggy area of land that gives way underfoot, often making progress difficult. It can also metaphorically mean a complex or difficult situation from which it is hard to extricate oneself.   Swamp, Morass, Marsh, Mire, Predicament, Dilemma   The political scandal turned into a quagmire that the government struggled to navigate.   مستنقع-مَأزِق

quantum   a discrete quantity or amount of something, particularly in physics, where it denotes the smallest possible discrete unit of any physical property.   Amount, Quantity, Unit, Particle   In quantum mechanics, particles exhibit behaviors that are fundamentally different from those observed in classical physics.   كمية

quell   suppress or put an end to something, especially by force. It can also mean to calm or pacify someone.   Suppress, Subdue, Quash, Squash, Calm, Pacify   The police were called in to quell the riots that erupted in the city center.   كَبَح-يَقْمَع

quilted   something that is stitched in a decorative pattern, usually with multiple layers of fabric and padding sewn together.   Padded, stitched, embroidered, cushioned.   She wrapped herself in a warm, quilted blanket on chilly evenings.   مُبَطَّن

querulous   someone who complains or grumbles often, especially in a peevish or petulant manner.   Complaining, Whining, Grumbling, Petulant,

Peevish   Her querulous tone during the meeting annoyed her colleagues, who found her constant complaints tiresome. مُتَذَمِّر

quintessential   the purest or most typical example of something; representing the most perfect or typical example of a quality or class. Classic, Model, Typical, Representative, Perfect   The film was hailed as the quintessential romantic comedy, capturing all the elements audiences love. الجوهري-مثالي

quiproquo   misunderstanding or confusion.   misunderstanding, confusing, misinterpretation, mistake.   The quiproquo arose from a miscommunication about the project deadline, leading to confusion among team members. سوء الفهم

quixotic   someone who is exceedingly idealistic, unrealistic, and impractical, often to the point of being unrealistic.   Idealistic, Romantic, Impractical, Unrealistic, Utopian   His quixotic belief that he could solve world hunger single-handedly led to disappointment when he realized the complexity of the issue. هَلْامُّوتِي-تَخَيُّلِي

quotidian   something that is ordinary, commonplace, or occurring daily.   Daily, Routine, Everyday, Commonplace, Mundane   Her quotidian tasks included grocery shopping and taking care of household chores. يَوْمِي

quotient   the result of dividing one quantity by another, especially in arithmetic. It can also mean a degree or extent of a quality or characteristic.

Result, Outcome, Division, Ratio   The quotient of 12 divided by 4 is 3.   الناتِج-حاصل قسمة

R r

racketeer   a person who engages in dishonest and fraudulent business dealings, often involving illegal activities like extortion or bribery.   Gangster, Criminal, Mobster, Extortionist, Fraudster   The authorities arrested the notorious racketeer who had been running a criminal organization in the city.
مُتَاجِر بِالذَّصدَب-مبتز

rake   1. a tool with a long handle and tines, prongs, used for gathering leaves or debris. 2. As a verb, it can mean to use a rake to gather something together.   1. Garden rake, Leaf rake, Hay rake. 2. Gather, Collect, Scoop up.   He spent the afternoon raking the fallen leaves from the yard into neat piles. المِجَرَّف

rakish   someone or something that is dashing, stylish, or slightly unconventional in appearance or behavior, often suggesting a carefree or debonair attitude.   Dashing, Stylish, Debbonair, Jaunty, Suave, devil may cry. He had a rakish charm about him, with his unbuttoned collar and tousled hair. أنيق-ماجِن-خَلَاعِي

ratification   the formal confirmation or approval of a proposed agreement, treaty, or contract, making it officially valid and legally binding.   Confirmation, Approval, Endorsement, Validation, Authorization   The ratification of the treaty required approval from all participating countries' legislatures. التصديق-إبرام-إقرار

ravenous   someone who is extremely hungry or famished, often showing an intense or insatiable appetite.   Famished, Starving, Voracious, Ravening, Hungry   After the long hike, they were ravenous and eagerly devoured the hot meal.
جَوْعان-مُفتَرِس-ذَهِم

readies   1. a verb form of READY, meaning to prepare or make something or someone ready. 2. As a noun, slang, readies refers to cash or money.   1. Prepares, Arranges, Organizes, Equips, Gears up. 2. Cash, Money, Funds, Currency.   She readies her equipment before every presentation to ensure everything goes smoothly.   يُجَهِّز

rearmament   the process of building up a new stock of military weapons and equipment, especially after a period of disarmament or reduced military capability.   Militarization, Remilitarization, Re-equipment, Re-equipping, Rebuilding of military forces. The government's rearmament program aimed to strengthen the country's defenses in response to growing regional tensions.   إِعَادَةُ التَّسَلُّح

recalcitrant   someone who is stubbornly resistant to authority, control, or discipline; uncooperative or defiant.   Uncooperative, Defiant, Insubordinate, Rebellious, Stubborn The recalcitrant student refused to follow the teacher's instructions, causing disruptions in the classroom.   عَاصٍ

recapitulate   to summarize and state again the main points of something. Summarize, Restate, Reiterate, Review, Outline   At the end of the meeting, the manager asked everyone to recapitulate their key takeaways from the discussion. يُلَخّص

receptivity   the willingness or ability to accept new ideas, suggestions, or experiences. Openness, Acceptance, Responsiveness, Willingness, Open-mindedness   Her receptivity to constructive criticism helped her improve her skills rapidly. تَقَبُّل

recidivism   the tendency of a convicted criminal to reoffend, especially repeatedly.   Reoffending, Relapse, Relapsing into crime, Habitual offending, Repetition of criminal behavior   Efforts to reduce recidivism include rehabilitation programs aimed at helping former inmates reintegrate into society. الإِنْتِكَاس الجَرِيمِي

recluse   a person who lives a solitary life and tends to avoid other people. Hermit, Solitary, Loner, Ascetic, Introvert   The old man was a recluse, rarely seen outside his remote cabin in the woods. مُنْعَزِل

recompense making amends to someone for loss or harm suffered; compensation or reward given for effort or work.   Compensation, Reward, Payment, Restitution, Remuneration   The company offered recompense to the affected customers for the inconvenience caused by the product recall. تَعْوِيض

reconcile   to restore friendly relations between, or to make two seemingly conflicting things compatible or consistent with each other.   Settle, Resolve, Harmonize, Mediate, Adjust After years of estrangement, the two brothers decided to reconcile and rebuild their relationship. يُصَالِح

reconnaissance	a military survey or exploration to gather information, especially to gain strategic knowledge about enemy forces or positions. Survey, Exploration, Scouting, Recon, Inspection	The soldiers carried out a reconnaissance mission to gather intelligence on the enemy's fortifications.	اسْتِطْلاَع

recumbent	describes a person or thing lying down or in a reclining position. Lying down, Reclining, Resting, Supine, Prone He preferred to read in a recumbent position, stretched out comfortably on the sofa.	مُسْتَلْقٍ

redounds	to contribute greatly to a person's credit or honor, or to result in something beneficial or detrimental.	Contribute, Result, Lead, Attribute, Affect	His hard work and dedication redound to the success of the entire project. يَؤُول-اِنْعَكَس على

redress	the act of setting right an unfair situation or wrong, or to compensation or remedy for a wrong or grievance.	Remedy, Correct, Rectify, Compensate, Reparation	The victims sought redress for the damages caused by the company's negligence.	تَعْويض-إِصلاح-تقويم

reeking	something emitting a strong, unpleasant smell.	Stinking, Smelly, Odorous, Foul, Malodorous	The garbage bin was reeking after several days in the hot sun.	مُنْتِن-يعبق ب

referendum   a general vote by the electorate on a single political question that has been referred to them for a direct decision.   Public vote, Plebiscite, Ballot, Poll, Popular vote   The government announced a referendum to decide whether the country should adopt a new constitution.   اِسْتِفْتَاء

regalement   the act of entertaining or providing enjoyment, often with lavish food and drink.   Entertainment, Amusement, Festivity, Hospitality, Feast   The host's regalement of his guests included a sumptuous banquet and live music.   إِكْرَام-تسلية-يمتع بالأطعمة والحديث المسلي

regurgitate   to bring swallowed food back up to the mouth, or to repeat information without understanding or analysis.   Vomit, Eject, Repeat, Recite, Parrot The student was able to regurgitate the facts during the exam but lacked a deeper understanding of the material.   يَتَقَيَّأ-يقول ما حفظه دون نقد او تحليل

reimburse   to repay someone for expenses they have incurred or to compensate someone for a loss or expense.   Repay, Refund, Compensate, Recompense, Pay back   The company agreed to reimburse her for the travel expenses she incurred during the business trip.   يُعَوِّض

relics   objects, often historical or religious, that have survived from the past, especially those held in reverence.   Artifacts, Antiquities, Heirlooms, Remnants, Remains The museum displayed ancient relics that provided insight into the culture and life of the early civilizations.   آثَار

relinquish   voluntarily give up or surrender something, such as a right, possession, or control.   Surrender, Give up, Abandon, Renounce, Cede   He had to relinquish his position as CEO due to health issues. يَتَخَلَّى

remedial   actions or measures taken to improve a situation, particularly in education, health, or correction of a problem or deficiency.   Corrective, Therapeutic, Restorative, Rectifying, Curative   The school offered remedial classes for students who needed extra help with their studies.   إِصْلاَحِي

remissness   a lack of care or attention to duty; negligence.   Negligence, Carelessness, Inattention, Laxity, Dereliction   His remissness in handling the project led to several critical errors that delayed the completion.   إِهْمَال-تَفريط-تَقصِير-تَهَاوُن

remnant   a small remaining quantity of something, often a leftover piece from a larger whole.   Remainder, Leftover, Residue, Fragment, Scrap After the sale, only a few remnants of fabric were left on the shelves.   بَقَايَا

remonstrance   a forcefully reproachful protest or objection.   Protest, Objection, Complaint, Reproach, Dissent   Despite their vigorous remonstrance, the board decided to proceed with the controversial policy.   اِحْتِجَاج

rend   to tear something into pieces forcefully or violently.   Tear, Rip, Shred, Split, Break   In a fit of rage, he tried to rend the letter into pieces. يَمْزِق

rendezvous   a planned meeting at a specific time and place, typically between two or more people.

Meeting, Appointment, Gathering, Assembly, Date   They agreed to a secret rendezvous at the café to discuss their plans. لِقَاء

renegade   a person who deserts and betrays an organization, country, or set of principles; one who behaves in a rebellious or unconventional manner.

Traitor, Defector, Rebel, Deserter, Turncoat The renegade soldier joined the enemy forces, causing outrage among his former comrades.   مُنْشَقّ-خَائِن-مُرْتَدّ

reparation   the making of amends for a wrong one has done, by paying money to or otherwise helping those who have been wronged.   Compensation, Amends, Restitution, Redress, Indemnity   The government agreed to provide reparations to the families affected by the wrongful actions of its officials. تَعْوِيض

repatriation   the process of returning someone to their own country. It can involve the return of refugees, soldiers, prisoners of war, or civilians to their homeland.

Return, Restoration, reinstatement, Homecoming, Reimmigration After several years abroad, the expatriate eagerly awaited his repatriation to his homeland, where his family and friends awaited him.   إِعادَةُ التَّوْطِين

repeal   the action of revoking or annulling a law, order, or agreement through official or legal means.

Abolition, Revocation, Annulment, Rescission
The government decided to repeal the outdated law, which had been in place for over a century.   إِلْغَاء

repentance   the action of feeling or expressing sincere regret or remorse for one's wrongdoing or sin.
Remorse, Regret, Contrition, Penitence
After realizing the consequences of his actions, he felt deep repentance and sought forgiveness from those he had wronged.   تَوْبَة

replete   being filled or well-supplied with something. It often implies a state of abundance or being well-stocked.   Filled, Full, Abundant, Brimming
The library was replete with books on every subject imaginable, providing a wealth of knowledge for the students.   مُمْتَلِئ

reprieve   a temporary relief from or postponement of a punishment, especially a death sentence. It can also mean any temporary relief from a difficult situation.
Pardon, Stay, Suspension, Respite   The governor granted a last-minute reprieve to the prisoner, halting the execution just hours before it was scheduled to take place.   إِرْتِيَاح

reprimand   a formal expression of disapproval, usually given by someone in authority.   Rebuke, Reproach, Admonishment, Censure The manager issued a stern reprimand to the employee for repeatedly arriving late to work.   تَوْبِيخ

reprisal   an act of retaliation, especially in a military context. It can also mean any act of revenge or counterattack. Retaliation, Revenge, Vengeance, Counterattack The country launched a military reprisal against its neighbor in response to the border incursion. اِنْتِقام

repudiate   reject or refuse to accept or be associated with something. It can also mean to deny the truth or validity of something. Reject, Renounce, Disown, Deny The politician was quick to repudiate the accusations of corruption, insisting that he was innocent of all charges. رَفْض

repugnance   intense disgust or aversion.   Disgust, Aversion, Loathing, Distaste   She felt a strong sense of repugnance at the sight of the spoiled food, turning away in disgust.   اِشْمِئْزاز

reputed   refers to being generally believed or considered to be a certain way, often based on reputation rather than confirmed fact.   Supposed, Alleged, Presumed, ApparentThe scientist was reputed to be one of the leading experts in her field, although her theories were sometimes controversial. مَزْعُوم

reputedly   refers to according to what is generally said or believed, often used to indicate that the information is based on reputation or hearsay rather than confirmed fact.   Supposedly, Allegedly, Apparently, Presumably   The old mansion was reputedly haunted, with many locals claiming to have seen ghosts there.   عَلَى ما يُزْعَم

requisite   something that is necessary for a particular purpose.   Necessary, Essential, Required,

Indispensable Possessing a valid passport is a requisite for international travel. ضَرُورِيّ

rescind to revoke, cancel, or repeal a law, order, or agreement.   Revoke, Cancel, Repeal, Annul   The company decided to rescind the job offer after discovering discrepancies in the candidate's application. إلْغاء

respite a short period of rest or relief from something difficult or unpleasant.   Relief, Break, Pause, Intermission   After hours of intense negotiations, both parties took a brief respite to regroup and consider their options. فَتْرَةُ راحَة

resuscitate to revive someone from unconsciousness or apparent death. It can also mean to make something active or vigorous again.   Revive, Revitalize, Restore, Reanimate   The paramedics worked tirelessly to resuscitate the drowning victim, eventually bringing him back to consciousness. إِنْعاش

reticence the quality of being reserved, restrained, or unwilling to speak freely.   Reserve, Shyness, Restraint, Taciturnity   His natural reticence made it difficult for him to share his thoughts and feelings with others. تَحَفُّظ-تَكَتُّم

reticent someone who is reserved, not inclined to speak freely, or is restrained in expression. Reserved, Withdrawn, Shy, Taciturn   She was reticent about her plans for the future, preferring to keep her ambitions to herself. مُتَحَفِّظ-تَكَتُّوم

retinue	a group of advisers, assistants, or others accompanying an important person. Entourage, Escort, Attendants, Suite	The queen arrived at the event with her retinue, each member playing a crucial role in the royal proceedings.	مُرافِقُون

retributive	punishment that is considered to be morally right and fully deserved, often reflecting a principle of justice where the punishment corresponds to the offense. Punitive, Vengeful, Penal, Retaliatory	The judge's decision was seen as retributive, aiming to ensure that the punishment fit the crime committed.	اِنْتِقَامِي

reveled	to take great pleasure or delight in something, especially in a lively and noisy way.	Celebrated, Enjoyed, Relished, Savored	They reveled in their victory, dancing and singing late into the night.	اِحْتَفَلُوا

reveling	taking great pleasure or delight in something, often in a lively and noisy manner.	Celebrating, Enjoying, Relishing, Savoring	The team was reveling in their hard-earned victory, with cheers and laughter echoing throughout the stadium.	اِحْتِفال-تَمَتَّع

revelry	lively and noisy festivities, especially when these involve drinking and dancing.	Celebration, Festivity, Merrymaking, Carousing	The New Year's Eve party was filled with revelry, as guests celebrated with music, dancing, and laughter until dawn.	اِحْتِفال صاخِب

reverie   a state of being pleasantly lost in one's thoughts; a daydream.   Daydream, Trance, Fantasy, Musing   She was lost in a reverie, imagining the adventures she would have on her upcoming vacation.   سَرْحَان

revved   to increase the running speed of an engine by pressing the accelerator, often to make the engine run more energetically or faster.   Accelerated, Sped up, Gunned, Raced   He revved the car's engine loudly, eager to start the race.   زَادَ سُرْعَةَ المُحَرِّك

rictus   a fixed grimace or grin, often implying a smile or expression that looks forced or unnatural. Grimace, Grin, Smirk, Sneer   The clown's painted face was stuck in a permanent rictus, giving him an eerie appearance.   تَكْشِيرَة

riding roughshod   to act with complete disregard for the feelings or rights of others, often behaving in an overbearing or oppressive manner.   Overbearing, Domineering, Bullying, Oppressive   The new manager was known for riding roughshod over employees' concerns, making decisions without any regard for their input. يَتَصَرَّفُ بِلا مُبالاة

rife   something widespread or abundant, especially something undesirable or harmful.   Widespread, Prevalent, Abundant, Common   The small town was rife with rumors after the unexpected events of the weekend.   مُنْتَشِر

rigmarole   a lengthy, complicated, and often unnecessary procedure or set of actions.   Nonsense, Hassle, Palaver, Bureaucracy, red tape.   The process to get a simple permit turned into a ridiculous rigmarole of endless paperwork and pointless meetings.
إِجْرَاءَات مُعَقَّدَة

rigorous   extremely thorough, exhaustive, or accurate; it can also mean harsh and demanding.
Thorough, Meticulous, Stringent, Strict   The scientist conducted a rigorous analysis of the data to ensure the results were accurate and reliable.
صارِم

riotous   characterized by wild and uncontrolled behavior; it can also refer to something very colorful and lively. Unruly, Disorderly, Boisterous, Turbulent   The celebration turned riotous, with people dancing in the streets and fireworks lighting up the sky.   صاخِب

risibility   the ability or tendency to laugh; it can also mean something that provokes laughter.
Laughter, Amusement, Hilarity, Mirth His natural risibility made him a favorite at parties, as he could easily make everyone laugh with his jokes.   قَابِلِيَّة لِلضَّحِك

roguery   behavior that is mischievous or dishonest, often in a playful or amusing way.
Mischief, Trickery, Deceit, Knavery   The old man's stories of his youthful roguery always brought a smile to the faces of his grandchildren.   مَكْر

rose-tinted   an overly optimistic or idealistic view of something, often ignoring its flaws or difficulties.
Idealized, Optimistic, Positive, Unrealistic   She viewed her childhood through rose-tinted glasses, remembering only the happy moments and forgetting the hardships.   نَظْرَة مُتَفَائِلَة-العمياء

rubicund   having a healthy reddish color, often associated with a rosy complexion.   Rosy, Ruddy, Florid, Red   After spending the day hiking in the fresh mountain air, his cheeks were rubicund with health.   مُحْمَر

ruckus   a noisy commotion or disturbance.   Commotion, Uproar, Hubbub, Tumult   The unexpected fireworks caused quite a ruckus in the neighborhood, with people rushing outside to see what was happening.   صَخَب

rueful   expressing sorrow or regret, especially in a slightly humorous or wry way.   Regretful, Sorrowful, Remorseful, Apologetic   With a rueful smile, he admitted his mistake and promised to make amends.   نَادِم

ruffian   a violent person, especially one involved in crime.   Thug, Hooligan, Bully, Hoodlum   The ruffian was well-known in the neighborhood for his frequent brawls and intimidating behavior.   بَلْطَجِي

rumination   the act of thinking deeply about something. It can also refer to the process by which ruminant animals, such as cows, chew their cud.   Contemplation, Reflection, Meditation,

Pondering, Pensiveness.   He spent the afternoon in quiet rumination, reflecting on the events of the past year and planning for the future.   تَأَمُّل

rumple   to make something untidy or wrinkled.   Crumple, Wrinkle, Crease, Muss   She quickly rumpled the sheets to make it look like someone had slept in the bed.   يُجَعِّد

ruses   actions intended to deceive someone; they are tricks or strategies used to mislead.   Tricks, Schemes, Deceptions, Stratagems   The spies employed various ruses to gather information without raising suspicion.   حِيَل

S s

sacristy   a room in a church where a priest prepares for a service, and where vestments and other things used in worship are kept.   Vestry, Sanctuary, Chapel, Sanctuary room   Before the ceremony began, the priest went to the sacristy to don his vestments and prepare for the mass. مَخْدَع القُدُس

saddled with   to be burdened or weighed down with a difficult responsibility or problem.   Burdened, Encumbered, Laden, Weighed down He was saddled with debt after the unexpected medical expenses. مُثْقَل بِـ

sagacious   having or showing keen mental discernment and good judgment; wise or shrewd.   Wise, Astute, Insightful, Prudent   Her sagacious advice helped the company navigate through the difficult economic times. حَكيم

salubrious   means health-giving; healthy, or pleasant and conducive to well-being. Healthy, Wholesome, Beneficial, Salutary   They moved to a more salubrious part of town, where the air was cleaner and the environment more conducive to their well-being. صِحّي

sanction   an official permission or approval for an action, or a penalty imposed to enforce compliance with a law or rule. Approval, Authorization, Consent, Penalty, Punishment, Restriction   The government imposed economic sanctions on the country in response to its aggressive actions. عُقُوبَة

sapphic   something related to lesbianism, often in a poetic or romantic context, originating from the poet Sappho and her work.   Lesbian, Homosexual (female), Romantic (female)   The poet's sapphic verses celebrated the beauty of love between women. سَـَافُّوي

sawdust   the tiny particles of wood produced by sawing, sanding, or cutting wood.   Wood shavings, Wood dust, Saw shavings   The floor of the workshop was covered in sawdust from the carpenters' work throughout the day.   نُشَارَةُ الخَشَب

scaffold   a temporary structure used to support work crews and materials to aid in the construction, maintenance, and repair of buildings, bridges, and other structures. It can also refer to a raised platform used for the execution of criminals.   Platform, Framework, Staging, Support structure   The workers erected a scaffold to reach the upper floors of the building for the renovation work.   سَقَالَة

scalped   the act of cutting or tearing a part of the human scalp, with hair attached, from the head, and generally occurred in warfare with the scalp being a trophy.   headed, decollated, guillotined, deskined. The barberous warrior scalped his victims with a swing of his knife.   مسلوخ فروة رأس

scant   barely sufficient or adequate; not enough in amount, quantity, or extent.   Insufficient, Meager,

Sparse, Limited   They had to make do with scant resources to complete the project on time. ناقِص-شحيح

scarlet   a bright red color that is slightly orange. Crimson, Vermilion, Red   She wore a stunning scarlet dress to the gala. قَرْمَزِي

schismatic   someone who promotes or engages in a division or separation from a larger group, especially within a religious or political context. Dissenter, Separatist, Sectarian, Heretic   The community was divided over the schismatic leader's call for a separate faction within the church. مُفَرِّق

scion   a descendant or heir, especially a young one of a noble family. Descendant, Heir, Offspring, Child As the scion of the wealthy family, he was expected to uphold their traditions and values. ذُرِّي

scoffed at   to mock or express contempt for something in a scornful or derisive manner. Mocked, Ridiculed, Dismissed, Derided   She scoffed at the idea that he could succeed without any prior experience. سْخَرِ مِن

sconces   decorative wall-mounted fixtures that hold candles or electric lights.   Wall bracket, Candle holder, Light fixture   The antique sconces added a touch of elegance to the hallway. قُرُبَاتٌ حَائِطِيّة

scouting   exploring an area to gain information, especially in a military or reconnaissance context. It can also refer to the activity of the Scouting movement, involving outdoor activities and community service for young people. Reconnaissance, Exploring, Surveying, Investigating   The scouting party moved silently through the forest, gathering intelligence on enemy positions.   استكشاف

scrawl   messy or hurried handwriting that is often difficult to read.   Scribble, Scratch, Jot, Messy writing   His scrawl on the note made it challenging to decipher his message.   خَطٌّ غَيْرُ مُرَتَّبٍ-يُخَرْبِش

scrounge   to obtain something, especially money or food, in a casual or informal way, often by searching or borrowing.   Beg, Borrow, Mooch, Cadge   He scrounged enough change from his friends to buy a coffee. التَذَقُّل

scruff   the loose skin at the back of the neck, especially on an animal, or can refer to a person's neck area, especially when it's unkempt or dirty.   Nape, Neck, Back of the neck   The dog was picked up by the scruff of its neck and gently placed in the crate.   المِنْطَقَةُ الخَلْفِيَّةُ لِلرَّقَبَةِ-قَفَا الْعُنُق

scrupulous   diligent, thorough, and extremely attentive to details, especially concerning moral or ethical standards.   Conscientious, Meticulous, Diligent, Precise   He was known for his scrupulous attention to every detail in his work, ensuring everything was done correctly.   دَقِيقٌ لِلْغَايَة

searing   something extremely hot or intense, often causing a burning sensation. It can also describe something that is emotionally or psychologically intense and deeply affecting. Burning, Scorching, Intense, Harrowing   The searing pain in his leg made it difficult for him to walk.   مُحْرِق

secretion   the process of producing and releasing a substance from a cell, gland, or organ for a specific purpose, often into the bloodstream or for external use.   Discharge, Release, Emission, Excretion   The gland's secretion of hormones regulates various bodily functions.   افراز

sediment   solid material that settles at the bottom of a liquid, often found in bodies of water or as residue from chemical reactions.   Deposit, Residue, Settling, Dregs   The sediment at the bottom of the riverbed contained layers of organic matter and minerals.   رَواسِب

servility   the quality or condition of being excessively submissive or obedient, often to an excessive or demeaning degree.   Subservience, Submissiveness, Obedience, Meekness   His servility towards his boss was evident in how he always agreed with everything she said, regardless of his own opinions.   المَذَلَّة

seigneur   historically refers to a feudal lord, especially in France under the Ancien Régime, or it can denote a man of rank or authority.   Lord, Nobleman, Baron, Feudal lord   The seigneur presided over the lands and estates with authority and feudal obligations.   سُدَيِّد

semblance   an outward appearance or resemblance to something, often implying a similarity that is not necessarily genuine or real.   Appearance, Likeness, Resemblance, Pretense   Despite their similar appearance, there was no semblance of familial relation between the two strangers.   مَظْهَر

senile   showing the physical and mental weaknesses associated with old age, especially in terms of memory loss and confusion.   Aged, Elderly, Doddering, Infirm   Her grandmother became increasingly senile in her final years, often forgetting familiar faces and events.شَيْخِي

sepultural   archaic of sepurchral, relates to a tomb, burial, or funeral, often describing something gloomy, dismal, or relating to death.   Funereal, Grave, Tomb-like, Mournful The sepulchral atmosphere of the cemetery added to the solemnity of the funeral service.   قَبْرِي

sepulture   the act or practice of burying the dead; burial. Burial, Interment, Entombment, Inhumation The family held a private sepulture ceremony for their beloved grandmother.الدَّفْن-ضريح

serendipity   the occurrence of events by chance in a happy or beneficial way.   Chance, Luck, Fortune, Happenstance Their meeting at the airport was pure serendipity, leading to a lifelong friendship. الصدفة السعيدة

serfdom   the state or condition of being a serf, a peasant who is bound to the land and subject to the will of the feudal lord.   Bondage, Feudalism, Slavery,

Subjugation   Serfdom was a common social structure in medieval Europe, where peasants worked the land in exchange for protection and sustenance.
عبودية العبيد-رِقّ-اِستِرقاق

sheath   a protective covering or case, typically for a blade or a part of the body, such as a knife sheath or a sheath for a sword.   Case, Covering, Scabbard, Holder   He carefully slid the knife back into its sheath after use.   غِمْد-جِرَاب

sheepishly   in a shy, embarrassed, or awkward manner, often due to feeling guilty or ashamed.   Timidly, Shyly, Awkwardly, Bashfully   He apologized sheepishly after realizing his mistake in front of everyone.   يِخْجِّل

shirk   avoid or neglect a duty or responsibility.   Avoid, Evade, Neglect, Dodge, sidestep, play truant from.   the negligible student manages to shirk from every homework assigned to him.   يتجنّب-يتهرب

shun   to deliberately avoid someone or something, often because they are disliked, considered dangerous, or unwelcome.Avoid, Reject, Ignore, Evade   She decided to shun social media for a while to focus on her studies.   تَجَذَّب-تَحَاشَى

sidestep   avoid or circumvent something, especially a problem or a difficult situation, often by taking indirect or evasive action.   Dodge, Evade, Avoid, Circumvent   He tried to sidestep the question by changing the topic of conversation.   تَفَادَى

siege a military operation in which an enemy force surrounds a town or building, cutting off essential supplies, with the aim of compelling those inside to surrender.   Blockade, Encirclement, Besiegement, Confinement The city endured a prolonged siege that lasted several months during the war.   حِصَار

sift   examine or sort through something thoroughly and carefully, often to separate out unwanted or important elements.   Filter, Strain, Screen, Sort   She sifted through the documents to find evidence of the fraud. غَرَّبَ-غَرْبَل-يُنَخِّلُ

sigil   a symbol or design considered to have magical or occult significance, often used in rituals or as a personal mark.   Seal, Symbol, Mark, Emblem   The wizard inscribed a sigil on the ground to ward off evil spirits.   خَاتَم

sillage the trail or scent left behind by a person wearing perfume or cologne as they move through the air.   trail, aura, dissipation of scent.   the scented candle left a perceptible sillage after it was put down.
أثر العطر ـأعقاب-بقايا الريح

simmering   cooking something gently at or just below the boiling point, typically allowing flavors to blend and develop slowly.   Stewing, Boiling gently, Cooking slowly The stew was left simmering on the stove for hours to enhance its flavors. الطهي الخفيف-ثَوَرَان-جَيَشَان

Simony   the act of buying or selling spiritual or church-related privileges, such as pardons or benefices.   buying of ecclesiastical preferent, purchase of church pardons and positions.   At that time, simony was widespread and priesthood could be bought.   شَرطَذَة-سِيمونية

sire   1. A respectful term for a male monarch or a father. 2. To father offspring, especially used in reference to animals. Father, Beget, Procreate, Monarch   1. The king, as sire of the realm, held significant authority over his subjects. 2. the sire is one of the country's top thoroughbred stallions.   السَّيِّد- أَنْجَب-مُنشِئ

skepticism   a questioning attitude or doubt towards knowledge, facts, or beliefs, often requiring evidence before accepting something as true. Doubt, Distrust, Disbelief, Suspicion, Incredulousness.   Scientific progress often thrives on healthy skepticism, challenging established theories to uncover new knowledge.   ّالشَّكّ

skirmish   a brief and usually small-scale fight or encounter between small groups of soldiers, often occurring before a larger battle or as part of a minor conflict.   Clash, Encounter, Scuffle, Fight   The soldiers engaged in a skirmish with enemy forces near the border.   اشتباك-مُنَاوَشَة

slapdash   something done hastily and without care, often resulting in a sloppy or careless outcome.   Careless, Hasty, Sloppy, Improvised   He submitted a slapdash report that was full of errors and poorly organized.   ّعَشْوائِي

sleuth   a detective or someone who investigates and solves crimes or mysteries.   Detective, Investigator, Gumshoe, Private Eye   The sleuth carefully examined the crime scene for any clues that might lead to the perpetrator.   مُحَقِّقٌ

slouch   1. To stand, sit, or walk with a drooping or hunched posture. 2. A posture or position where one's body is drooping or hunched forward.   1. Laze, Linger, Sag, Stooge. 2. Droop, Hunch, Posture.   He tended to slouch in his chair during long meetings, much to the annoyance of his boss.   الإنحناء-تَدَلَّى

slue   or slew, as a verb, means to turn or rotate quickly, especially in a different direction.   Swerve, Veer, Pivot, Swing   The car slued off the road after hitting a patch of ice.   تَدَوَّلَ بِسُرْعَةٍ-انعطاف

sluicing   washing or rinsing something with a stream of water or other liquid, often to clean or separate materials.   Washing, Rinsing, Flushing, Cleaning   They were sluicing the dirt off the vegetables before cooking them.   غَسْلٌ بِالتَّدْفِق

sniggering   laughing in a disrespectful, suppressed, or derisive manner, often at something perceived as amusing or embarrassing.   Snickering, Chuckling, Sneering, Smirking   She couldn't help but notice their sniggering whenever she made a mistake during the presentation.   الضَّحِك السَّاخِر

sniveling   crying or sniffing in a feeble, whining, or self-pitying manner.   Whining, Sniffling, Sobbing, Mewling, crying.   Despite his sniveling, he managed to persuade his parents to let him stay up late. الذّحَيق-بكاء

soar   fly or rise high in the air with little effort, often suggesting a swift and majestic movement. Glide, Ascend, Fly, Rise   The eagle soared effortlessly above the mountains, searching for prey. طَارَ-يحلق

sobriquet   a nickname or a descriptive name given to a person, often highlighting a particular characteristic or trait. Alias, Moniker, Nickname, Title   His sobriquet The Rocket, reflected his speed and agility on the basketball court. لَقَب

sojourn   a temporary stay or visit, typically for a short period of time.   Visit, Stay, Stopover, Residence   During their European sojourn, they visited several countries and explored different cultures. زِيَارَةٌ مُؤَقّدَة

soliciting   asking for or trying to obtain something from someone, typically through persuasion, requests, or advertisements.   Requesting, Asking, Entreaty, Pleading   He was caught soliciting donations outside the grocery store. التّسَدوُّل

solicitude   care, concern, or attention given to someone or something.   Concern, Care, Attention, Thoughtfulness   She showed great solicitude towards her elderly neighbor, regularly checking in on her and offering assistance. الاهْتِمام

solipsism   the philosophical idea that only one's own mind and experiences are certain to exist or that one's own existence is the only real or true existence.

Egoism, Subjectivism, Self-centeredness His solipsism made it difficult for him to empathize with others' perspectives. الأنانية

solitaire   1. A card game played by one person, typically involving arranging cards in a particular order or pattern. 2. a diamond or other gem set in a piece of jewellery by itself.   Gem, Jewel, Diamond   1. She passed the time playing solitaire on her computer during the long flight. 2. she wore a beautiful diamond solitaire.   الصُّبْرِيّة-فَرداني-قطعة الماس

solvency   the ability of an individual or organization to meet its financial obligations and debts as they become due. Financial stability, Creditworthiness, Fiscal health   The company's improved profitability ensured its long-term solvency and ability to expand. القُدْرَةُ عَلَى السَّدَادِ-ملاءة مالية

sombre   or Somber, describes something that is dark, gloomy, or melancholy in mood, tone, or atmosphere.   Gloomy, Melancholy, Dismal, Dark The funeral was a sombre occasion, with everyone dressed in black and speaking in hushed tones. كَئِيب

soothsayer   a person who claims to have the ability to foresee or predict the future, often through supernatural or mystical means.   Prophet, Seer, Oracle, Diviner   The ancient soothsayer predicted a bountiful harvest for the coming year based on celestial observations. عَرَّاف

sordid   something morally shameful, dirty, or squalid, often involving immoral or unethical behavior.
Dirty, Filthy, Disgraceful, Repulsive   The scandal revealed the sordid details of the politician's corrupt dealings.   بَشِع

spasmodic   something that occurs irregularly or intermittently, often in sudden bursts or fits. Irregular, Intermittent, Fitful, Occasional   Her spasmodic efforts to study resulted in inconsistent academic performance. تَشَنُّجِي

spawning   the process of producing or depositing eggs, especially in large quantities, often used in the context of fish or other aquatic organisms.
Reproducing, Breeding, Generating, Producing
The salmon return to the river each year for spawning.   تَفَرُّخ

spectre   also spelled specter, refers to a ghostly or haunting image, especially one that is seen as a sign or warning of something to come.   Ghost, Apparition, Phantom, Spirit   The old castle was said to be haunted by the spectre of a long-dead knight.   شَبَح

spoonerism   a linguistic phenomenon where the initial sounds or letters of two or more words are swapped to create a humorous or sometimes nonsensical effect.
lapsus linguae, slip of the tongue.   his friends laughed when he said a blushing crow instead of a crushing blow, it was a funny spoonerism.   تلعثم-تبادل خاطئ للأصوات

sporadic   something that occurs irregularly, infrequently, or scattered in intervals.Occasional, Intermittent, Irregular, Scattered   They experienced sporadic power outages throughout the month due to the stormy weather.   مُتَفَرِّق

spurious   something that is not genuine, authentic, or true; often used to describe something that is deceitful or falsely presented.False, Fake, Bogus, Counterfeit   The company was accused of selling spurious products that did not meet safety standards.   زَائِف

spurns   to reject, refuse, or disdainfully turn away from something or someone.   Rejects, Refuses, Disdains, Declines   She spurned his offer of reconciliation after their argument.   يَرُدُّ-اِسْتَنْكَف عن- أَزْهَى

squalor   a condition of being extremely dirty, unpleasant, or sordid, often associated with poverty or neglect.   Filth, Dirtiness, Sordidness, Degradation   The abandoned building was in a state of squalor, with trash scattered everywhere and broken windows.   بَذْرَة-بؤس-بَذاذَة

squeamish   someone who is easily nauseated or disgusted, especially at the sight or thought of something unpleasant or morally objectionable.   Nauseated, Queasy, Nervous, Skittish   She's quite squeamish and can't even watch horror movies without feeling sick.   سَرِيعُ الغَثَيَان

squelsh	to make a soft, sucking sound, typically when walking on wet ground or when something wet is pressed or squeezed. Squish, Slop, Splash, Splosh They heard the squelch of their shoes as they walked through the muddy field.	صْدُوفِلْش

squirming	the present participle of the verb squirm, which means to wriggle or twist the body from side to side, usually because of nervousness or discomfort.	Wriggling, Wiggling, Fidgeting, Twisting	The children were squirming in their seats during the long and boring lecture.	يِتَلَوّى

staid	someone who is serious, steady, and respectable in behavior, often implying a somewhat reserved or conservative demeanor. Sedate, Sober, Dignified, Serious	His staid demeanor made him well-suited for the role of a judge.	مُتَزَن

stalemate	a situation in which neither side in a conflict or competition can make progress or gain an advantage, resulting in a deadlock.	Deadlock, Standstill, Impasse, Gridlock The negotiations reached a stalemate when neither party would compromise on their demands.	مَأْزُوْق

stammer	to speak with sudden involuntary pauses and repetitions of words or syllables due to nervousness or a speech disorder.	stutter, falter, hesitate, stumble	He began to stammer when asked to speak in front of a large audience.	يَتَأْتَـأُـتَـعَـثّر

stead	a place or position that someone or something occupies. It is often used in the phrase "in someone's stead," meaning "instead of someone." Place, Position, Role, Spot He took charge of the meeting in his boss's stead while she was on vacation.

مَوْضِع

steadfastness   the quality of being firm, unwavering, and resolute in purpose or belief, often despite difficulties or obstacles.   Firmness, Resoluteness, Determination, Perseverance Her steadfastness in pursuing her dreams eventually led to her success. الاستِقامَة-ثَبَات-رُسُوخ

stealth   the act of moving, proceeding, or acting in a covert or secretive manner, intending not to be noticed or detected.   Secrecy, Clandestine, Covert, Sneaky, furtive. The cat moved with stealth, silently creeping towards its prey.   التَّخَفِّي

stifled   to suppress, restrain, or suffocate something, typically an emotion, sound, or action.   Suppress, Quash, Muffle, Smother   She stifled a yawn during the long and boring lecture. كَبِت

stipend   a fixed regular sum of money paid to someone, typically to support their living expenses or to cover incidental expenses.   Allowance, Grant, Payment, Subsistence   As an intern, she received a modest stipend to help cover her transportation costs. مُنَحَة-أُجرَة-راتِب

stipulate   to demand or specify a requirement, typically as part of an agreement, contract, or condition.   Specify, Demand, Require, Set   The contract stipulates that the work must be completed by the end of the month. يشترط-حَدّد-يُشِيرُ إلَى

straddling   sit or stand with one leg on either side of something, or to be positioned across or between two things. Spanning, Crossing, Extending over, Overlapping   The new highway bridge is straddling the valley, providing a vital link between the two towns. فَرشَدَة-تفحيج

stratified   to arrange or divide into layers or strata, often based on different levels or categories.
Layered, Segmented, Tiered, Graduated   The society was stratified into distinct social classes based on wealth and status. طَبَقِي-مُرَتّب

stridency   the quality or state of being loud, harsh, or grating in sound or tone.   Shrillness, Harshness, Loudness, Discordance   The stridency of her voice made it difficult to concentrate on the lecture.
صَوْتٌ عَالٍ وَجَافّ-صدَرير

strode   is the past tense of stride, which means to walk with long, decisive steps in a specified direction.
Marched, Walked, Stepped, Tramped   He strode across the room with confidence to deliver his speech.   خَطَا

stultification   the act of making someone or something appear foolish or absurd, or causing something to lose enthusiasm and initiative, especially through restrictive or tedious procedures.   Frustration, Hampering, Hindrance, Suppression The endless bureaucracy led to the stultification of the employees' creative ideas. تَجهِيل-تسفيه

stupefaction   a state of being stupefied, which is characterized by extreme astonishment, shock, or a state of near-unconsciousness.   Amazement, Bewilderment, Astonishment, Daze   The sudden news left him in a state of stupefaction, unable to comprehend what had happened. ذُهُول

stupefied   a state of shock or astonishment, or having dulled senses due to being overwhelmed or stunned.   Dazed, Shocked, Astonished, Bewildered   She was stupefied by the unexpected news and could hardly believe what she was hearing. مَذْهُول

stymied   to be prevented or hindered from progressing or achieving something. Blocked, Thwarted, Hindered, Obstructed   Their plans for expansion were stymied by the new regulations imposed by the government. مُحْبَط

subdue   to overcome, quieten, or bring under control a feeling or person.   Conquer, Defeat, Suppress, Quell   The police had to use force to subdue the rioters and restore order. قَمَع

sublet   to lease or rent all or part of a property that is already leased or rented from someone else.
Lease, Rent out, Sublease   She decided to sublet her apartment while she was working abroad for a year. تَأْجِير فَرْعِي

sublimate   to divert or modify an instinctual impulse into a culturally higher or socially more acceptable activity. It can also refer to the process where a solid changes directly into a gas without passing through the liquid state.   Channel, Redirect, Transfer, Divert   She sublimated her anger into creative writing, producing some of her best work during that period.   تَسَامَى

subordination   the act of placing someone or something in a lower rank or position in relation to another.   Inferiority, Subjection, Subjugation, Submission   The company's strict hierarchy emphasized the subordination of employees to their managers.   التَّبْعِيَة

suborn   to bribe or induce someone to commit an unlawful act, especially to commit perjury which is lying under oath.   Bribe, incite, instigate, induce, procure   The lawyer was accused of attempting to suborn a witness to give false testimony in court.   يُحَرِّضُ عَلَى الإِدْلَاءِ بِشَهَادَةٍ زُور

subpar   below an average or expected standard. Inferior, mediocre, below average, poor, second-rate   The team's performance was subpar, leading to their early elimination from the tournament.   دُونَ الْمُسْتَوَى الْمُتَوَقَّع

subsist   to maintain or support oneself, especially at a minimal level; to continue to exist or remain in being.   Survive, endure, exist, persist, live   The villagers subsist on the limited crops they

can grow during the short growing season. يَعِيشُ-
يَسْتَمِرُّ-يَبْقَى

subsistence   the action or fact of maintaining or supporting oneself at a minimal level; the means of supporting life, typically at a basic level.   Survival, existence, livelihood, sustenance, maintenance Many families in the region depend on subsistence farming to meet their daily needs.   كَفَاف-مُقَوِّمَاتُ
الْحَيَاة

subsume   to include or absorb something in something else, often in a way that it becomes part of a larger or more comprehensive entity. Include, incorporate, absorb, encompass, assimilate, engulf The new policy will subsume existing regulations under a more unified framework.   يُشْمَل-ُ يَضُمُّ- يَسْتَوْعِب

subterfuge   a deceit used in order to achieve one's goal; a trick or dishonest way of achieving something.   Deception, trickery, deceit, evasion, ruse   The spy used subterfuge to gain access to the guarded facility. حِيلَة- خُدْعَة- مُرَاوَغَة

sullen   showing irritation or ill humor by a gloomy silence or reserve; bad-tempered and sulky. Morose, sulky, gloomy, dour, glum   After losing the game, he sat in the corner with a sullen expression on his face.
عَبُوس - مُكْتَئِب - مُتَجَهِّم

supercilious   behaving or looking as though one thinks they are superior to others.   Arrogant, haughty, condescending, disdainful, patronizing   Her supercilious attitude made it difficult for her to make friends at the new school. ‎مُتَغَطْرِس - مُتَكَبِّر - مُتَعَجْرِف

superciliousness   the quality or state of behaving as though one thinks they are superior to others.
        Arrogance, haughtiness, condescension, disdain, patronization His superciliousness was evident in the way he talked down to his colleagues. ‎غَطْرَسَة - تَكَبُّر - تَعَجْرُف

supererogate   to do more than is required, ordered, or expected.   Exceed, surpass, overperform, outdo, go beyond   The employee chose to supererogate by staying late and completing tasks that were not part of his job description.   ‎يَتَجَاوَزُ الْمَطْلُوبَ - يُؤَدِّي أَكْثَرَ مِمَّا يُطْلَبُ مِنْه

supererogation   the act of performing more than is required by duty, obligation, or need. Excess, surplus, overachievement, additional effort, extra work   Her supererogation in helping the community went beyond what anyone expected, earning her much admiration.
‎تَجَاوُزُ الْمَطْلُوبِ - أَدَاءٌ فَوْقَ الْوَاجِب

supererogatory   actions that go beyond what is required or expected, especially in moral or ethical terms. Excessive, extra, nonessential, unnecessary, surplus   His donation to the charity was supererogatory, as he had already fulfilled his obligations.   ‎فَوْقَ الْمَطْلُوبِ - تَطَوُّعِيّ - زَائِد عَنْ الْحَاجَة

supersede   to take the place of a person or thing previously in authority or use; to replace.   Replace, succeed, supplant, overtake, displace   The new software update will supersede the old version, offering improved features and better performance.   يَحِلُّ مَحَلَّ - يَسْتَبْدِلُ - يُبْدِل

suppletion   the occurrence of an unrelated form to fill in gaps in a paradigm, particularly in the inflection of verbs and nouns, e.g., went as the past tense of go.   Replacement, substitution, alternative form, irregular form, complementary form   The verb "to be" is an example of suppletion in English, with forms like "am," "is," "was," and "were" not being derived from the same root.   اِسْتِبْدَال - تَكْمِيل - تَعْوِيض

surfeit   an excessive amount of something; an overabundant supply or indulgence. Excess, overabundance, surplus, glut, profusion   The guests were treated to a surfeit of food and drink at the lavish banquet.   إِفْرَاط - زِيَادَة - فَيْض

surmised   to suppose that something is true without having evidence to confirm it; to guess.   Guessed, hypothesized, assumed, inferred, conjectured   She surmised that he was not feeling well because he had not shown up to work for three days.   خَمَّنَ - ظَنَّ - اِفْتَرَض

surreptitious   kept secret, especially because it would not be approved of; done by stealth. Secret, clandestine, stealthy, furtive, covert   The two coworkers exchanged surreptitious glances during the meeting to avoid drawing attention.   سِرِّيّ - خَفِيّ - مُتَخَفِّ

surreptitiously   in a way that attempts to avoid notice or attention; secretively.   Secretly, clandestinely, stealthily, furtively, covertly   He surreptitiously slipped the note into her bag without anyone noticing.

بِسِرِّيَّةٍ - بِخِفِّيَّةٍ - بِتَخَفّ

surrogate   a substitute, especially a person deputizing for another in a specific role or office.   Substitute, proxy, replacement, stand-in, alternate   When the primary actor fell ill, the director called in a surrogate to take over the role.   بَدِيل - وَكِيل - ذَائِب

sustenance   food and drink regarded as a source of strength; nourishment. It can also mean the maintaining of someone or something in life or existence.   Nourishment, food, nutrition, sustenance, livelihood   The hikers packed enough sustenance to last them through their week-long journey in the mountains.   غِذَاء - قُوت - مَعِيشَة

svelte   slender and elegant, describing a person. Slender, slim, graceful, lithe, willowy She looked stunning in the svelte black dress at the evening gala.

رَشِيق - ذَحِيف - أَنِيق

swindle   to use deception to deprive someone of money or possessions.   Cheat, defraud, deceive, trick, con   The con artist tried to swindle the elderly couple out of their life savings.   يَحْتَال - يَغُشّ - يُخْدَع

swoop   to move rapidly downward through the air, especially in an attack; it can also mean to come down upon something in a sudden, swift attack.   Dive, descend, plummet, pounce, sweep   The eagle will swoop down to catch its prey with incredible speed and precision.   يُنَقْضّ - يَهْبِطُ بِسُرْعَةٍ - يَنْدَفِع

symbiotic   a mutually beneficial relationship between two different organisms, people, or groups.   Mutualistic, cooperative, interdependent, reciprocal, synergistic The clownfish and the sea anemone have a symbiotic relationship, each providing benefits that help the other survive.   - تَعَايُشِيّ - تَكَافُلِيّ - تَعَاوُنِي

synchronism   the simultaneous occurrence or existence of events or actions; the state of being synchronous.   Simultaneity, concurrence, coincidence, synchronicity, synchronization   The synchronism of the dancers' movements was impressive, as they moved in perfect harmony with each other and the music.   تَزَامُن - تَزَامُنِيَّة - تَزَامُنِي

syndication   the act of selling a piece of content, such as a television show or a column, for publication or broadcasting in multiple places simultaneously.   Distribution, circulation, dissemination, broadcasting, publication   The popular comic strip achieved greater fame through syndication, appearing in newspapers across the country.   تَوْزِيع - تَشْتِيت - تَعْميم

T t

tacit   understood or implied without being stated openly; implicit.   Implicit, unspoken, implied, understood, unstated   There was a tacit agreement among the team members that they would support each other in times of need.   ضِمْنِيّ - مُتَّفَق عَلَيْهِ ضِمْنًا - مُلَمَّح

taciturnity   the state or quality of being reserved or reticent in conversation; the trait of being habitually silent or uncommunicative.   Reticence, silence, reserve, quietness, aloofness   His taciturnity was often mistaken for arrogance, but he was simply a person of few words.   قِلَّةُ الْكَلاَم - تَحَفُّظ - صَمْت

talons   the sharp, hooked claws of a bird of prey.   Claws, nails, hooks   The eagle's talons gripped the branch firmly as it scanned the area for potential prey.   مَخالِب

tandem   two or more things arranged one behind the other, or working together simultaneously.   Together, in line, consecutively, jointly, in sequence   The two cyclists rode in tandem, drafting off each other to conserve energy during the long race.   بِالتَّوَازِي - عَلَى التَّوَالِي - مُتَتَالِيًا

tantamount to   equivalent in seriousness to; virtually the same as.   Equivalent to, equal to, synonymous with, comparable to, on par with   Her refusal to answer the question was tantamount to an admission of guilt.   مُعَادِل لِـ - مَكَافِئ لِـ - يُعْتَبَر كَـ

tartar   a hard calcified deposit that forms on the teeth and contributes to their decay. It can also refer to a member of various Mongolic and Turkic peoples who, in the Middle Ages, inhabited large parts of Central Asia and Eastern Europe. Calculus in a dental context, plaque, deposits, scale in a dental context. Regular dental cleanings are necessary to remove tartar buildup and maintain oral health.   الجير

tatter   a torn and ragged piece of cloth or clothing. Rag, shred, fragment, piece, scrap   His old coat was worn to tatters after years of hard use.   خِرْقَة -
قِطْعَة مُمَزَّقَة - قُماش مُمَزَّق

taxidermy   the art of preparing, stuffing, and mounting the skins of animals with lifelike effect.
        Animal preservation, stuffing, mounting, specimen preparation The museum's natural history exhibit features several examples of expert taxidermy.
        تَحْنِيطُ الْحَيَوانَات

tedium   the state of being tedious; long, slow, or dull, and tiresome.   Boredom, monotony, weariness, ennui, dullness   The tedium of the long meeting made it hard for her to stay focused. رَتَابَة - مَلَل - ضَجَر

teetotaller   a person who abstains from consuming alcoholic beverages. Abstainer, non-drinker, temperance advocate, sober individual
Despite the festive atmosphere, he remained a teetotaller and enjoyed the party with a glass of sparkling water.   مُمْتَنِع عَنِ الشُّرْب -
رَافِض لِتَدَاوُلِ الْكُحُول

telos   an ultimate objective or aim, particularly the end goal of a process or the ultimate purpose of something.   Goal, purpose, aim, end, objective   For Aristotle, the telos of human life is to achieve eudaimonia, or flourishing and happiness.   الْغَايَة - الْهَدَف - الذِّهَايَة

tempested   subjected to or characterized by a violent storm or tempest.   Stormed, battered, besieged, buffeted, lashed   The small fishing village was tempested by the sudden and fierce storm, leaving many homes damaged.   مُعَرَّض لِلْعَاصِفَة - مُتَضَرِّب بِالْعَاصِفَة

temporal   worldly as opposed to spiritual affairs; relating to time.   Secular, worldly, earthly, mundane, profane   The priest emphasized the importance of focusing on spiritual matters over temporal concerns.   زَمَنِيّ - دُنْيَوِيّ - وَقْتِي

tenancy   the possession of land or property as a tenant. Leasehold, rental, occupation, lease, rentingThe couple entered into a tenancy agreement for a small apartment near the city center.   حَقّ الإِيجَار - الإِيجَار - الإِسْتِئْجَار

tenement   a room or a set of rooms forming a separate residence within a house or block of apartments, typically one that is run-down and overcrowded.   Apartment, flat, residence, dwelling, lodgingMany families lived in cramped and unsanitary conditions in the old tenement buildings of the city.   شَقَّة - مَسْكَن - عِمَارَة

tenor   1. the general meaning, sense, or content of something. 2. In music, it refers to the highest of the ordinary adult male singing voice or the second lowest of the standard four voice types.   1. sense, theme, gist, substance. 2. Singer, vocalist, male alto.   The tenor of his speech was one of optimism and hope for the future.   مَعْنَى - مَغْزًى - جَوْهَر - تَذْنُور - مُغَنٍّ - مُؤَدِّي

tenterhooks   a state of anxious suspense or unease.   Anxiety, suspense, agitation, nervousness, anticipation   She was on tenterhooks waiting for the results of her medical tests.   عَلَى أَحْرَ مِنَ الْجَمْر - فِي حَالَةٍ مِنَ التَّوَتُّرِ - فِي حَالَةٍ مِنَ الْقَلَق

tenure   the holding or possessing of something, such as property, an office, or a position. In an academic context, it often refers to a permanent post.   Occupancy, possession, term, incumbency, ownership   After years of dedicated teaching and research, she was finally granted tenure at the university.   حِيَازَة - فَتْرَة وِلَايَة - تَوَلٍّ دَائِم

theocracy   a form of government in which a deity is recognized as the supreme civil ruler, and religious leaders govern in the deity's name.   Religious rule, ecclesiocracy, clerical governance   In a theocracy, the laws of the state are based on religious principles and scriptures.   حُكْم دِينِيّ - ثِيُوقْرَاطِيَّة

throttled   to have choked or strangled someone; it can also refer to the act of controlling or limiting the amount or speed of something.   Choked, strangled, suffocated, restricted, constrained   The engineer

throttled the engine to prevent it from overheating.
ْخَذَقَ - خَذَقَ، قَلَّلَ الذَّدَفُّق - حَدَّ مِن

thudded to have made or caused a dull, heavy sound, typically one made by an object falling to the ground. Pounded, crashed, banged, knocked, hit The book thudded to the floor, breaking the silence of the library. أَحْدَثَ صَوْتَ ارْتِطَام - ارْتَطَم

thwart prevent someone from accomplishing something or to oppose successfully. Hinder, obstruct, impede, prevent, frustrate The detective's quick thinking helped thwart the criminal's plan to rob the bank. يُحْبِط - يُعَرْقِل - يَمْنَع

timber wood prepared for use in building and carpentry. It can also mean trees grown for wood. Wood, lumber, logs, planks, boards The cabin was built from timber harvested from the nearby forest. أَخْشَاب - خَشَب - أَشْجَار الغَابَة

timorous showing or suffering from nervousness, fear, or a lack of confidence. Fearful, timid, shy, apprehensive, hesitant The timorous student hesitated before answering the teacher's question, afraid of making a mistake. خَائِف - وَجِل - مُرْتَبِك - خَجُول

tincture 1. a medicine made by dissolving a drug in alcohol, or a slight trace of something. 2. a slight trace of something. 3. alcoholic drink. Solution, extract, infusion, essence, trace 1. The herbalist prepared a tincture of echinacea to help boost the immune system. 2. she could not keep a tincture of bitterness out of her voice.   صَبْغَة - قَطْرَة - أَثَر طَفِيف

tintinnabulation   the ringing or sound of bells. Ringing, chiming, pealing, tinkling, tolling   The tintinnabulation of the church bells echoed through the valley on Sunday morning.   رَنِينُ الأَجْرَاس - صَدَوْتُ الأَجْرَاس

tirade   a long, angry speech of criticism or accusation.   Diatribe, rant, harangue, outburst, denunciation   The coach launched into a tirade after the team lost the match due to careless mistakes.   خِطَاب غَاضِب - تَوْبِيخ شَدِيد - كَلاَم لاذِع

titillate   to stimulate or excite someone, especially in a sexual way.   Arouse, excite, tease, stimulate, tantalize   The novel contained passages that were intended to titillate the readers.   يُثِير - يُلْهِب - يُحَفِّز

toadies   people who flatter or ingratiate themselves with someone important in order to gain favor or advantage.   Sycophants, flatterers, bootlickers, brown-nosers, fawners   The CEO was surrounded by toadies who constantly praised his decisions, hoping to secure promotions.   مَتَزَلِّقُون - مُتَمَلِّقُون - مُتَذَلِّلُون

tongs   a tool used for gripping and lifting objects, consisting of two long arms that are joined at one end and open and close like pincers or scissors. Pincers, tweezers, forceps, nippers, grippers She used tongs to turn the hot coals in the barbecue grill.   مِلْقَط - مَسَكَّة - كَلاَّبَة

topple to fall forward, as from having too heavy a top; to overthrow or defeat. Overturn, overthrow, tumble, collapse, unseat The strong winds caused the tree to topple over, blocking the road. يُسْقِط - يُطِيح - يُسْقِط مِنَ السُّلْطَة

topsy-turvy in a state of confusion or disorder. Chaotic, disorganized, messy, jumbled, muddled After the children finished playing, the room was left in a topsy-turvy state. فَوْضَوِيّ - غَيْر مُنَظَّم - مُبَعْثَر

torpor a state of physical or mental inactivity; lethargy. Lethargy, sluggishness, inertia, dormancy, apathy The bear enters a state of torpor during the winter months, conserving energy until spring. خُمُول - كَسَل - سُبَات

torrid very hot and dry; it can also refer to something full of difficulty or tribulation, or to passionate emotions, especially in a romantic context. Scorching, sweltering, blistering, intense, fervent The desert's torrid climate made it challenging for the explorers to continue their journey. حَارّ جِدًّا - مُلْتَهِب - مَحْمُوم

tranquilizer a drug used to reduce tension or anxiety. Sedative, calmative, depressant, relaxant, anti-anxiety medication The veterinarian administered a tranquilizer to the anxious dog before the surgery. مُهَدِّئ - مُسَكِّن - مُرَخٍّ

transgress   to violate a law, command, or moral code; to go beyond the bounds or limits of what is considered acceptable.   Violate, breach, infringe, overstep, trespass   The student was disciplined for transgressing the school's code of conduct.   يَتَجَاوَز - يَخْتَرِق - يَنْتَهِك

transient   lasting only for a short time; impermanent. Temporary, fleeting, short-lived, ephemeral, transitory   The beauty of a sunset is transient, fading away within moments.   مُؤَقَّت - زَائِل - عَابِر

translunary   something situated beyond or above the moon; celestial or otherworldly.   Celestial, extraterrestrial, ethereal, heavenly, unearthly   The poet wrote about a translunary realm, filled with wonders beyond human comprehension.   فَوْقَ الْقَمَر - سَمَاوِي - فَوْقَ الأَرْضِي

traverse   to travel across or through something.   Cross, navigate, journey, travel, pass through   The hikers planned to traverse the entire mountain range over the course of a week.   يَعْبُر - يَجْتَاز - يَسِيرُ عَبْر

tremulously   in a way that is characterized by trembling or shaking, often due to nervousness, fear, or weakness.   Shakily, quiveringly, fearfully, nervously, unsteadily   She spoke tremulously during her first public speech, her hands shaking slightly as she gripped the podium.   بِارْتِجَاف - بِارْتِعَاش - بِرَجْفَة

trenchant   vigorous or incisive in expression or style; having a sharp edge in a literal or figurative sense. Incisive, sharp, penetrating, cutting, acute The critic's trenchant review left no doubt about his disdain for the movie. لاذِع - حَادّ - قَاطِع - نافِذ

trepidation   a feeling of fear or anxiety about something that may happen. Fear, apprehension, dread, anxiety, unease   As the deadline approached, she felt a growing sense of trepidation about the project.   قَلَق - خَوْف - اِضْطِرَاب - هَلَع

tribunal   a court of justice or any person or institution with authority to judge, adjudicate on, or determine claims or disputes.   Court, panel, judiciary, board, committee   The tribunal convened to hear the cases of the accused war criminals.   مَحْكَمَة - هَيْئَةُ تَحْكِيم - لَجْنَةُ قَضَائِيَّة

troglodytism   the practice or condition of living in caves or living in seclusion and ignorance. Caveman lifestyle, cave dwelling, seclusion, isolation, reclusiveness   The isolated village was accused of troglodytism, with inhabitants living without modern amenities and knowledge.   الْمَعِيشَة فِي الْكُهُوف - الْعَزْلَة - النَّزْعَة إِلَى الْبَدَائِيَّة

truculent   eager or quick to argue or fight; aggressively defiant. Belligerent, hostile, aggressive, combative, confrontational   His truculent behavior at the meeting made it difficult for any constructive dialogue to take place.   عُدْوَانِيّ - شَرِس - مُشَاكِس - جَادِل

trudging   walking slowly and with heavy steps, typically because of exhaustion or harsh conditions.
        Plodding, slogging, lumbering, shuffling, dragging   After a long day at work, she found herself trudging home through the snow.   يَمْشي بِتُثَاقُل
ُ- يَتَثَاقَل فِي المَشْي - يَجُرُّ أَقْدَامَه

tryst   a private, romantic rendezvous between lovers.
        Rendezvous, meeting, assignation, date, liaison
        The couple arranged a secret tryst in the park under the cover of darkness.   لِقَاء حَميمي - مَوْعِد غَرَامي
- مَقَابَلَة سِرِّيّة

tsarism   a system of government in which a tsar (emperor) has absolute power and authority, typical of the Russian Empire before the 1917 revolution. Autocracy, absolute monarchy, despotism, dictatorship, authoritarianism   Tsarism in Russia ended with the abdication of Tsar Nicholas II and the subsequent revolution in 1917.   النِّظَامُ الْقَيْصَرِيّ - النِّظَامُ الْمَلَكِيّ الْمُطْلَق

tumultuous   making a loud, confused noise; uproarious or characterized by disorder and chaos.
        Chaotic, turbulent, disorderly, uproarious, riotous
        The crowd gave a tumultuous applause after the thrilling concert.   صَاخِب - فَوْضَوِيّ - مُضْطَرِب - هَائِج

turpitude   depravity; a base or vile character or behavior.   Degeneracy, corruption, wickedness, immorality, evil   His actions were filled with such moral turpitude that he was expelled from the organization.   الفُسُوق

tycoon a wealthy and powerful businessperson or industrialist, especially one who controls a large enterprise. Magnate, mogul, baron, captain of industry, entrepreneur He started as a small-time entrepreneur and eventually became a media tycoon with investments across multiple industries. صَاحِب أَعْمَال نَاجِح

U u

ubiquitous   present, appearing, or found everywhere.
Omnipresent, ever-present, pervasive,
widespread, universal In today's digital age,
smartphones have become ubiquitous, with almost
everyone owning one. وَاسِع الاِنتِشَار

umbrage   1. offense or annoyance, usually as a
result of a slight or insult. 2. shade or shadow,
especially as cast by trees.   Offense, irritation,
resentment, displeasure, indignation She took umbrage
at his comments, feeling they were disrespectful and
uncalled for.   استياء

unanimity   a state or condition of complete
agreement or unity among a group of people.
Consensus, agreement, harmony, accord,
concordance   The decision was reached with unanimity
among the board members, reflecting their shared
vision for the company's future.   الإِجْمَاع

unbecoming   not appropriate or fitting; not suitable
for a particular person or situation.   Inappropriate,
unfitting, improper, indecorous, unseemly   His
unbecoming behavior at the formal dinner offended
many of the guests.   غَيْر مُلاَئِم

unbeknownst   without the knowledge of someone.
Unknown to, unaware, ignorant of, oblivious to
Unbeknownst to her, he had been planning a
surprise party for her birthday.   دُونَ أَنْ تَعْلَم

unbridled   unrestrained; not controlled or limited.
     Uncontrolled, unrestrained, unchecked, unrestricted, wild   Her unbridled enthusiasm for the project was contagious, inspiring the entire team.   غَيْر مَكْبُوب

unchaperoned   without a chaperone; not accompanied or supervised by an adult or responsible person.   Unsupervised, unattended, alone, unaccompanied   She was uncomfortable attending the party unchaperoned, knowing it could lead to gossip.   دُون مُرَافِق

uncouth   lacking good manners, refinement, or grace; awkward or clumsy in appearance or behavior.   Crude, rude, rough, boorish, uncivilized   His uncouth behavior at the formal dinner embarrassed his companions.   غَلِيظ الأُخْلاق

uncreased   something that is smooth and without folds or wrinkles.   Smooth, unwrinkled, flat, pristine   She carefully ironed the shirt until it was completely uncreased.   غَيْر مَجْعَّد

underlet   leasing or renting property at a rate below the market value or the rate that could be obtained under current market conditions.   sublease, sublet He decided to underlet his apartment to a friend temporarily, charging a lower rent than usual.   تأجير بسعر أقل

undermine   to weaken or impair gradually or insidiously; to sabotage or diminish the strength, effectiveness, or confidence in someone or something.

Sabotage, weaken, subvert, erode, undercut   His constant criticism began to undermine her self-confidence. يُقَوِّض

underscoring   emphasizing or highlighting the importance or significance of something, often through repeated mention or emphasis.   Emphasizing, highlighting, stressing, accentuating, reinforcing   The professor's comments were aimed at underscoring the need for thorough research in the field.   تَسْلِيط الضوء على

unduly   excessively, inappropriately, or beyond what is reasonable or proper.   Excessively, overly, unreasonably, excessively, disproportionately   She was unduly harsh in her criticism of his work, considering it was his first attempt.   بِشَكْلٍ غَيْر مُعَقَّل

unequivocal   leaving no doubt; clear and unambiguous.   Clear, definite, explicit, unambiguous, categorical   His unequivocal statement of support reassured everyone of his commitment to the project. بَلا شُكّ - وَاضِح بِشَكْلٍ لا لِبْسَ فيه

unerringly   in a way that is consistently accurate or without error; infallibly.   Infallibly, accurately, precisely, correctly, flawlessly   She has an uncanny ability to unerringly predict market trends. بِدَقَّةٍ لا تُضَاهَى

unfeigned   genuine; sincere; not feigned or pretended.   Genuine, sincere, heartfelt, authentic, real   Her unfeigned enthusiasm for the project inspired the entire team. حَقِيقِي

ungallant   to behavior that is not courteous or chivalrous, often implying a lack of manners or politeness, especially towards women.   Rude, discourteous, impolite, disrespectful His ungallant behavior towards the hostess offended the guests at the dinner party. بشكل غير أنيق

unilateral   involving or done by only one side or party; affecting only one side. One-sided, single-sided, independent, solo   The decision to relocate the company's headquarters was made unilaterally by the CEO, without consulting the board. أحادي

unkempt   untidy or disheveled in appearance. Messy, disheveled, untidy, scruffy, sloppy   After a long day of hiking, he returned home with unkempt hair and dirty clothes. مُهمل-أَشعَث

unperturbed   not disturbed or troubled; calm and serene despite difficulties or problems.   Calm, composed, unruffled, undisturbed, serene   She remained unperturbed by the criticism, confident in her own abilities. هادئ

unremunerative   describes something that does not provide financial gain or reward; it is not profitable or financially beneficial. Unprofitable, non-remunerative, unrewarding, unprofitable   His hobby of collecting rare stamps proved to be unremunerative despite his passion for it. غير مربح

unscrupulous   describes a person or behavior that is dishonest or unethical, often willing to act illegally or immorally to achieve their goals.   Dishonest, unethical, immoral, corrupt, deceitful The unscrupulous businessman exploited loopholes in the law to avoid paying taxes. غَيْر أَخْلَاقِي

unstinting   given or giving generously and without restraint.   Generous, unselfish, bountiful, unsparing, lavish   Her unstinting support for the charity has made a significant difference in many lives. سَخِي

unsubstantiated   not supported or proven by evidence.   Unproven, unsupported, baseless, groundless, unwarranted   The rumors about the new policy changes are unsubstantiated and should not be taken seriously. غَيْر مُسْتَنَد

unsurpassable   unable to be exceeded in quality, achievement, or extent.   Unbeatable, incomparable, matchless, supreme, unrivaled   The beauty of the sunset over the mountains was unsurpassable, leaving everyone in awe.   غَيْر قَابِل لِلتَّفَوُّق

untenable   not able to be maintained or defended against attack or objection, usually referring to a position or argument. Indefensible, unsustainable, weak, flawed, unviable   The lawyer realized that his client's alibi was untenable and would not hold up in court. غَيْر قَابِل لِلدِّفَاع

untrammeled   not restricted or restrained; free to act or move without hindrance.   Unrestrained, unrestricted, unhampered, free, unfettered   The artist's creativity was untrammeled, allowing her to explore new and innovative techniques. غَيْرُ مُقَيَّد

unwarily	without caution or awareness; in a way that shows a lack of carefulness.	Carelessly, heedlessly, recklessly, incautiously, thoughtlessly	He unwarily left his wallet on the table, making it an easy target for thieves. بِغَيْرِ حَذَر

unwavering	steady and resolute; not changing or becoming weaker in determination or purpose.	Steadfast, resolute, determined, firm, unyielding	Her unwavering commitment to her studies resulted in her graduating at the top of her class. ثَابِت

upbraiding	to scold or criticize someone severely.	Reprimanding, rebuking, chastising, reproaching, berating	The manager gave an upbraiding to the employee for repeatedly missing deadlines. تَأْنِيب

upstart	a person who has risen suddenly to wealth or high position, especially one who behaves arrogantly.	Parvenu, newcomer, social climber, self-made man/woman, arriviste, neophyte, nouveau riche, vulgarian, Johnny come lately.	The seasoned executives were not pleased with the upstart who quickly climbed the corporate ladder. حديث النعمة

urbanely	in a sophisticated, polished, and suave manner.	Smoothly, suavely, elegantly, gracefully, refinedly	He spoke urbanely, charming everyone at the dinner party with his wit and grace. بِأُسْلُوب مُتَحَضِّر

urchin   a mischievous young child, especially one who is poorly or raggedly dressed.   Ragamuffin, waif, street child, imp, scamp   The little urchin darted through the crowded market, laughing as he dodged the shopkeepers. وَلَد شَقِي

usurer   a person who lends money at unreasonably high rates of interest. Loan shark, moneylender, extortionist, financier, Shylock   The struggling farmer fell into the clutches of a usurer who charged exorbitant interest rates.   مُرَابٍ ـآكِل الربا

usurper   a person who takes a position of power or importance illegally or by force.   Seizer, interloper, pretender, impostor, dethroner   The usurper seized the throne, overthrowing the rightful king in a swift and brutal coup. مُغْتَصِب

usury   the practice of lending money at unreasonably high rates of interest. Loan-sharking, exploitation, extortionate lending, predatory lending   The government's new regulations aim to crack down on usury and protect borrowers from unfair lending practices.   الرِّبَا

V v

vacillate to waver between different opinions or actions; to be indecisive. Waver, hesitate, dither, fluctuate, oscillate She tended to vacillate between studying engineering and pursuing a career in art, unable to make a firm decision. يَتَرَدَّد

vacuous having or showing a lack of thought or intelligence; mindless.Empty, blank, unintelligent, inane, foolish His vacuous comments during the meeting revealed his lack of understanding of the topic. فَارِغ

vagaries unexpected and unpredictable changes in a situation or someone's behavior.Whims, caprices, quirks, fluctuations, whimsies The vagaries of the weather made it difficult to plan outdoor events in advance. تَقَلُّبَات

vagrancy the state of living as a vagrant; homelessness, especially when it involves begging. Homelessness, vagabondage, wandering, transient lifestyle The city's new policies aimed to address the issue of vagrancy by providing more resources for the homeless. تَشَرُّد

vagrant a person without a settled home or regular work who wanders from place to place and lives by begging. Drifter, wanderer, vagabond, transient, homeless person The kind-hearted man offered food and shelter to the vagrant he found sleeping on his porch. مُتَشَرِّد

vague   not clearly expressed, understood, or perceived; lacking in detail or precision.   Unclear, ambiguous, indistinct, hazy, obscure Her instructions were so vague that no one understood what needed to be done.   غَيْر وَاضِح

valence   the capacity of an atom or a group of atoms to combine with other atoms, measured by the number of electrons it can share, lose, or gain.   Combining capacity, bonding capacity, chemical potential   The valence of carbon is four, allowing it to form up to four covalent bonds with other atoms.   تَكَافُؤ

vanguard   the leading part of an advancing military formation or the forefront of an action or movement.   Forefront, spearhead, front line, leading edge, cutting edge   The vanguard of the revolution consisted of young, passionate activists demanding change.   طَلِيعَة

vantage   a place or position that gives a good view of something or a comprehensive perspective.   Viewpoint, position, standpoint, perspective, outlookFrom his vantage point on the hill, he could see the entire city spread out below him.   نُقْطَة إِشْرَاف ـ أَفضَلِيّة

varmint   a troublesome or mischievous person or animal, often used to describe a pest.   Pest, nuisance, rascal, scoundrel, rogue   The farmer set traps to catch the varmint that was stealing his chickens.   حَيَوَان مُؤْذٍ

vehemence   the display of strong feelings, passion, or intensity.   Passion, intensity, fervor, forcefulness, ardor   She spoke with such vehemence about the injustice that it moved everyone in the room. حِدَّة

velocity   the speed of something in a given direction.   Speed, swiftness, rapidity, pace, rate   The scientist measured the velocity of the moving object to calculate its momentum.   سُرْعَة

veneration   great respect or reverence for someone or something. Reverence, respect, admiration, awe, esteem   The community's veneration for the elderly teacher was evident in the large turnout at her retirement ceremony. تَبْجِيل

verandah   a roofed platform along the outside of a house, level with the ground floor.   Porch, terrace, balcony, patio, deck   They enjoyed their morning coffee on the verandah, overlooking the garden.   شُرْفَة

verbatim   in exactly the same words as were used originally; word for word.   Word-for-word, exactly, precisely, literally, faithfully   She repeated the instructions verbatim to ensure there were no misunderstandings. حَرْفِيًّا

verbosity   the quality of using more words than needed; wordiness. Wordiness, prolixity, long-windedness, loquacity, circumlocution   The professor's verbosity made his lectures difficult to follow and understand. إِسْهَاب

verdict   a decision on a disputed issue in a civil or criminal case or an inquest.   Judgment, decision, ruling, finding, conclusion   The jury delivered a guilty verdict after deliberating for several hours. حُكْم

verily   truly or certainly.   Indeed, truly, certainly, surely, really.   Verily, I say unto you, the truth will set you free.   حَقًّا

veritable   being truly or very much so; often used to emphasize a description.   Real, genuine, true, actual, bona fide   The garden was a veritable paradise, filled with blooming flowers and singing birds.   حَقِيقِي

vernacular   the language or dialect spoken by the ordinary people in a particular country or region.   Dialect, colloquial language, everyday language, regional language, common speech The novel was written in the vernacular of the region, making it relatable to local readers.   لُغَة العَامَّة

vertiginous   1. causing or experiencing a sensation of dizziness or having a high, steep ascent. 2. relating to or affected by vertigo. Dizzying, giddy, whirling, spinning, high The vertiginous cliffs made her feel lightheaded just by looking at them. دُوَارِي

vestibule   an antechamber, hall, or lobby next to the outer door of a building.   Entrance hall, lobby, foyer, hallway, atrium Guests were asked to wait in the vestibule before being escorted to the main hall.   رِوَاق

vestigial   forming a very small remnant of something that was once much larger or more noticeable; having a function that has become diminished or lost over the course of evolution.   Residual, leftover, rudimentary, atrophied, remaining   The appendix is often considered a vestigial organ, with little to no function in the human body.   أَثَرِيّ-ضَامِر

vetoed   to reject or prohibit a decision or proposal made by a law-making body.   Rejected, overruled, disallowed, blocked, negated   The president vetoed the bill, sending it back to Congress for further revisions.   مَرْفُوض-يرفض

vexed   feeling or showing irritation, annoyance, or distress.   Annoyed, irritated, troubled, exasperated, aggravated   She was vexed by the constant noise from the construction site next door.   مُنْزَعِج

viable   capable of working successfully or feasible.   Workable, feasible, practical, achievable, attainable   After extensive research, they concluded that solar energy was a viable solution for the community's power needs.   قَابِل لِلتَّطْبِيق-حيوي

vicissitudes   the changes and fluctuations, often unexpected and difficult, that occur in life or fortune.   Changes, variations, fluctuations, twists, turns   Despite the vicissitudes of his career, he remained optimistic and resilient.   تَقَلُّبَات

victual food or provisions, typically as prepared for consumption.   Provisions, food, sustenance, nourishment, supplies The travelers stocked up on victuals before embarking on their long journey.
مَؤُوذَة

victualling   the process of supplying food or provisions, especially for ships or troops.   Provisioning, supplying, catering, stocking, equipping   The ship's crew spent the morning victualling the vessel for its long voyage.   تَمْوِين

vignette   a brief evocative description, account, or episode; it can also refer to a small illustration or portrait that fades into its background without a definite border.   Sketch, portrait, depiction, scene, illustration The author included a vignette in the novel that beautifully captured the protagonist's childhood. لَوْحَة قَصِيرَة

villanelle   a highly structured 19-line poem with two repeating rhymes and two refrains, consisting of five tercets followed by a quatrain.   Poetic form, verse, poem The poet crafted a beautiful villanelle that captured the essence of love and loss.   قَصِيدَة
الفِيلاَّنِيل

virility the quality of having strength, energy, and a strong sex drive; manliness.   Manliness, masculinity, potency, vigor, robustness   The ancient statue was often admired for its depiction of the warrior's virility and power. فُحُولَة

virtuosity   great skill in music or another artistic pursuit.   Skill, expertise, proficiency, mastery, artistry The pianist's virtuosity was evident in her flawless performance of the complex concerto. بَرَاعَة

virtuoso a person highly skilled in music or another artistic pursuit. Maestro, prodigy, expert, master, genius The young violinist was a virtuoso, captivating audiences with her extraordinary talent. فَذَّان بَارِع

visitation an official or formal visit, especially one for the purpose of inspection or supervision. Inspection, visit, tour, survey, examination The school prepared for the annual visitation by the accreditation committee. زِيَارَة رَسْمِيَّة

vista a pleasing view, especially one seen through a long, narrow opening. View, panorama, prospect, outlook, scene From the top of the hill, they enjoyed a breathtaking vista of the valley below. مَنْظَر

vitriolic filled with bitter criticism or malice. Acerbic, scathing, venomous, caustic, bitter The politician's speech was vitriolic, attacking his opponent with harsh and spiteful words. لَاذِع

vivacity the quality of being attractively lively and animated. Liveliness, exuberance, energy, enthusiasm, spiritedness Her vivacity and charm made her the center of attention at every party. حَيَوِيَّة

vocation a strong feeling of suitability for a particular career or occupation. Calling, profession, occupation, mission, career   She felt a deep vocation to become a nurse and help those in need. مَهْنَة

vocational   an occupation or employment, particularly one involving specialized skills or training.   Occupational, professional, technical, trade-related, job-related   He enrolled in a vocational school to learn carpentry and gain practical skills for his career.   مَرهْنِي

vociferation   loud or vehement shouting or calling.   Clamor, uproar, outcry, yelling, shouting   The heated debate was filled with vociferation as each side tried to make their point heard.   صِيَاح

vociferous   expressing feelings or opinions in a very loud or forceful way.   Boisterous, clamorous, outspoken, noisy, vehement   The protesters were vociferous in their demands for justice, making their voices heard throughout the city.   صَاخِب

volatility   the tendency to change rapidly and unpredictably, especially for the worse.   Unpredictability, instability, variability, fluctuation, turbulence The volatility of the stock market makes it a risky investment for those seeking stability.   تَقَلُّب

volleys   a series of utterances, questions, or actions delivered in rapid succession; in sports, it refers to hitting or kicking a ball before it touches the ground.   Barrage, burst, salvo, stream, onslaught   The journalist faced volleys of questions from the eager

reporters as soon as she stepped out of the courtroom.
وَابِل

vouchsafe   grant or give something to someone in a
gracious or condescending manner. Confer, bestow,
grant, deign, offer   The king vouchsafed an audience
to the humble petitioner, listening to his plea with a kind
ear.   يُمْنَح

vulture   a large bird of prey with a bald head,
feeding mainly on carrion. It can also metaphorically
refer to a person who preys on or exploits others.
Scavenger, predator, exploiter, opportunist The
vultures circled high above, waiting for their chance
عُقَاب-شخصٌ جَشِعٌ وحشيّ

waded   walk through water or another substance that impedes movement. Trudged, plodded, slogged, splashed, forded   They waded through the shallow river to reach the other side. خَاضَ

wail   to make a prolonged, high-pitched cry of pain, grief, or anger.Cry, howl, lament, moan, sob The child began to wail loudly when she couldn't find her mother in the crowded store. يُصْرِح

walloped   to hit someone or something very hard.   Thrashed, whacked, pounded, smacked, clobbered   He walloped the punching bag with all his strength, releasing his pent-up frustration. إِضَرَبَ بَعُنْف

wallow   to roll about or lie in mud or water, especially to keep cool or for pleasure; it can also mean to indulge in an unrestrained way in something pleasurable.   Indulge, bask, luxuriate, immerse, revel   After a stressful week, she allowed herself to wallow in a hot bath for hours.   يَتَمَرَّغ-انغماس

wan   looking pale and giving the impression of illness or exhaustion. Pale, pallid, ashen, sickly, washed-out   After several sleepless nights, he appeared wan and fatigued. شَاحِب

waning   decreasing in size, extent, or degree; becoming weaker or less vigorous.   Diminishing, decreasing, dwindling, fading, declining   The waning

moon cast a dim light over the quiet landscape.
مُتَذَاقِص-ارتِرَدَاد-انحِدَار

waylay   to stop or interrupt someone and
detain them in conversation or trouble them in some
other way.   Ambush, accost, intercept, surprise,
detain The reporter attempted to waylay the celebrity
as she exited the restaurant, hoping for an exclusive
interview.   يَعتَرِض-تَرَبَّص

waywardly   In a way that is difficult to control or
predict because of unusual or perverse behavior.
        Erratically, unpredictably, capriciously   He
acted waywardly, refusing to follow any rules.
        بِطَريقَةٍ شَاذَّة

waywardness   Difficult to control or predict because
of unusual or perverse behavior.   Unruliness,
unpredictability, capriciousness   Her
waywardness made her a challenging student to teach.
        شَذَاذَة

weltering   1. moving in a turbulent or chaotic
manner, often used to describe being soaked or
drenched. 2. lie soaked in blood.   Swirling, tumbling,
seething, rolling, tossing   After the heavy rain, the
fields were a weltering mess of mud and water.
        تَخَبُّط-تَقَلُّب

wherewithal the means or resources especially
financial needed for a particular purpose.   Resources,
means, ability, capability, funds   He did not have
the wherewithal to buy a new car, so he decided to
repair the old one.   الإمْكَانِيَّات

whim a sudden or capricious idea or desire.   Fancy, impulse, caprice, notion, urge   On a whim, she decided to take a spontaneous trip to the beach.   نَزْوَة

wielding   holding and using a tool or weapon effectively; it can also mean having and being able to use power or influence.   Handling, brandishing, manipulating, exercising, utilizing   The knight was skillfully wielding his sword in battle, demonstrating his expertise.   يُسَيْطِر

willow   a type of tree or shrub with slender, flexible branches and narrow leaves, often found near water.   Salix   The graceful branches of the willow tree swayed gently in the breeze by the riverside.   صَفْصَاف

window-dressing   the act of making something appear more attractive than it really is, often through superficial or deceptive means.   Facade, embellishment, decoration, superficiality, pretense The company's impressive financial report turned out to be mere window-dressing, hiding its actual poor performance. تَجْمِيل ظَاهِرِي

withered-up   dried or shriveled, often due to lack of moisture or age.   Shriveled, dried-up, desiccated, wilted, shrunken   The plants in the neglected garden were all withered-up and brown from the prolonged drought.   مُتَسَرِّم-ذَابِل

withheld   to keep something such as information, money, or emotions back or retain it. Retained, kept back, reserved, concealed, suppressed   She withheld the truth from her parents to avoid hurting their feelings.   امتَنع-مَحجُوب

Z z

zeugma   a figure of speech in which a word
applies to two others in different senses
        example: she broke his car and his heart.
العبارة الجامعة

9 798333 119773